JUSTICE
under the
RUBBLE

JUSTICE
under the
RUBBLE

THE SALVATION ARMY
BUILDING COLLAPSE

ANDREW STERN ESQ.
with George Anastasia

CAMINO BOOKS, INC.
Philadelphia

Manufactured in the United States of America

1 2 3 4   22 21 20 19

Cataloging-in-Publication data available from the Library of Congress, Washington, DC.

ISBN 978-1-68098-027-1

ISBN 978-1-68098-028-8 (ebook)

Interior design: P. M. Gordon Associates, Inc.

Cover design: Jerilyn Bockorick

This book is available at a special discount on bulk purchases for educational, business, and promotional purposes. For information write:

Publisher
Camino Books, Inc.
P.O. Box 59026
Philadelphia, PA 19102
www.caminobooks.com

To Gwen and Our Children,
Eric, Jeff and Jen

JUSTICE
under the
RUBBLE

CHAPTER ONE

THE LAST BODY WAS pulled out shortly after 11 p.m. That's what John O'Neill, the Philadelphia Fire Department captain who was overseeing the rescue operation, thought when he ordered his men to take a break.

"It was quite warm," O'Neill would recall while describing the rescue work that had begun late on the morning of June 5, 2013, and had continued long into the night. Dozens of highly trained workers had spent hours working through a massive pile of rubble that was once a Salvation Army Thrift Store located on the corner of 22nd and Market Streets in Philadelphia.

"Everybody was pretty much drained," O'Neill said. "It was hot. Everybody's dusty and dirty."

Rescue teams—firefighters and EMTs trained for that kind of work—had been at it for more than twelve hours. At that point, no one knew all the details of what had happened. But it didn't really matter. For those on site, the only issue was rescue. Wade through all the rubble and look for bodies. Hope that maybe somebody was still alive under the debris. But twelve hours into the operation, O'Neill knew that finding anyone alive was unlikely.

While technically this was still a rescue operation, "extrication"— getting the bodies out—was the reality. The rescue teams had found six corpses. The first was a woman named Kimberly Finnegan. She was thirty-five and was recently engaged to be married. It was her first day working the register at the Salvation Army Thrift Store.

Her body was pulled out at 1:30 p.m., three hours after a four-story, unsupported and unstable wall that was part of a poorly planned and executed demolition job collapsed onto the roof of the Thrift Store.

It happened in a flash.

There was a strange sound, a whoosh that seemed to suck the air out of the city block, witnesses would recall, and then the wall of the partially demolished structure was gone. A cloud of dust swept over the site and out onto Market Street, like a brief, blinding desert windstorm whipping across the heart of a city. Tons of brick, concrete, wood and debris rained down on the roof of the Salvation Army building, a one-story structure with a basement. The store, which anchored the corner of 22nd and Market Streets, was hard up against the unsupported wall. In fact, its chimney ran up that wall. The roof of the shop collapsed under the weight of the falling debris. It was 10:41 a.m. on a bright, sunny Wednesday morning. The store had been open about an hour.

The first Wednesday of every month is Salvation Army "Family Day," a day of discounts and sales, a day when the Salvation Army anticipates high shopping volume. This particular store was a favorite for customers who liked to hunt for buys and bargains. The store attracted shoppers from all parts of the city because of its location. It was on the fringe of the Rittenhouse Square neighborhood, an area of expensive high-rise apartments, condos, stately old brownstones and turn-of-the-century townhouses populated by some of the wealthiest residents in Philadelphia. Many donated their "old" and "used" clothes, household appliances and "bric-a-brac" to the thrift shop. On Family Day, a Salvation Army worker would later explain, "almost all the stuff in the store is half price."

And the "stuff," a Salvation Army official would say, was "very good-quality material."

Indeed, the store generated serious income. It was, to put it simply, a moneymaker. Estimates were that, "per square foot," it was the most profitable in the Salvation Army region that included Philadelphia and its suburbs. That economic issue would later figure into a debate about why the store hadn't been closed after high-ranking members of the charitable organization were warned about the potential dangers being posed by the demolition next door.

In fact, on May 22, 2013, two weeks before the collapse, an email that would later surface in criminal and civil litigation warned of the "threat to life and limb" the demolition work posed and cautioned that, if action were not taken, everyone involved would be looking at "headlines none of us want to read."

Those headlines were being written while John O'Neill caught his breath and gave his men a break after they had pulled out the body of Roseline Conteh. She was fifty-two, the mother of nine, an immigrant from Sierra Leone who had come to the United States ten years earlier.

She lived in the Kingsessing neighborhood of Southwest Philadelphia, a couple of miles from the store. She worked as a nursing assistant after coming to America to find a better life for herself and her family. She loved bargain hunting, and the Salvation Army Thrift Store was one of her favorite haunts.

O'Neill, a seasoned veteran of rescue operations who would later become a Battalion Chief, had worked in this kind of situation many times. In fact, he had been sent up to New York during the 9/11 crisis, when he spent ten days dealing with the worst catastrophe in American history. He was a clean-shaven man with focus and purpose. He had a genuine care and concern for every single victim and a keen understanding of the effect of tragedy—especially of those of this magnitude. He was more shocked by finding life than by discovering death.

What lay in front of him, while hardly the size or scope of the Twin Towers collapse, would nonetheless become an infamous burial site in Center City Philadelphia.

"Very similar characteristics, just on a smaller scale," he would tell a jury.

"We had brick . . . unreinforced masonry, construction brick," he said. "There was cinderblock. There was wood, timber, joists, asphalt from the flat roof. . . . We had to go through various layers to get to each of the people we were trying to recover."

There was a rescue dog, a brown Lab, on scene in Philadelphia. But the problem, O'Neill said, was that in a situation like this one "a human scent has a way of traveling along open air." Another problem was clothing. Rescuers often look for clothes while digging through the debris of a building collapse. Bright colors are often signs of life amid the rubble. Someone wearing a red shirt or a blue jacket would stand out against the dusty gray, white and brown debris under which they were buried.

But this was a store full of clothing, much of it, like the victims, buried in the pile. That added to the difficulty as rescuers tried to sift through the collapse. Another major problem was not knowing how many people were inside when the wall came down and how many had gotten out.

Throughout the day, as word spread and as news reports blared on radios and TVs, people came to the site. Family members who knew, or feared, that loved ones had been in the store joined the crowd. The media were providing live reports. This was a highly trafficked area.

There was a subway entrance on the corner of 22nd and Market just in front of the entrance to the thrift shop. A recently opened luxury high-rise condominium stood on the other side of Market Street along with a high-end supermarket. And, as the crowds gathered, according to at least some reports, lawyers began showing up, some donning their own hardhats, along with litigation construction experts. This was an unspeakable tragedy, one of the worst building collapses in the history of the city. But for some who practiced in the personal injury field, it was also a reality that for every victim there would be a lawsuit.

In the end, nineteen victims or representatives of their estates would file. Those suits would be consolidated and become the basis for one of the longest and most dramatic civil trials held in the Commonwealth of Pennsylvania. The civil trial would take place in a large, stately courtroom on the sixth floor of the iconic City Hall building at Broad and Market Streets, just eight blocks from where John O'Neill stood on that warm night watching, listening and wondering as his men regrouped.

O'Neill knew that several victims who had gotten out shortly after the collapse were alive and in the hospital. The reports were that most of them would survive. He also knew about those who had not.

Kimberly Finnegan's had been the first body taken out. O'Neill thought Roseline Conteh's might be the last. The body of Borbor Davis, a sixty-eight-year-old Liberian immigrant who worked part-time at the store and had been sorting clothes in the basement, had been located at 7:54 p.m. At 8:15 rescuers extracted the remains of Juanita Harmon, a seventy-five-year-old grandmother who had stopped in the Thrift Store that morning after paying her electric bill at the PECO (Pennsylvania Electric Company) office on 22nd Street. Then around 10 p.m. rescuers found the bodies of Mary Simpson and Anne Bryan. The two young women, both twenty-four, were friends who had decided to spend the day bargain shopping. Simpson had just started a career as an audio engineer.

Anne Bryan, whose mother, Nancy Winkler, was the City Treasurer of Philadelphia, had just finished her first year at the Pennsylvania Academy of the Fine Arts. She had gone bicycle riding with her mother earlier that day and planned to go with her friend to the Salvation Army shop, where she would donate some clothes. Then they would spend the rest of the morning hunting for bargains. They got there at a little after 10 a.m. They were inside when the wall collapsed. Sifting through clothes in the middle of the store, they had no chance to get out.

Other than the victims, the major players in the drama were the demolition contractor, the architect who had hired him and who was supposed to be overseeing the work, the businessman who owned the properties being demolished, and the Salvation Army. All would become defendants in the civil suits that followed and at different times would point fingers at one another, trying to shift blame and responsibility as more and more details were made public.

It didn't have to happen. That's what anyone who took the time to analyze the building collapse would come to believe. But the unanswered question remained—who was *really* at fault? There were so many opportunities to avoid the tragedy, but none had been taken. Instead, power, greed, indifference and hubris created a situation that led to death, grievous injuries and destruction. Those responsible had been warned repeatedly in the weeks leading up to tragedy.

But they chose to disbelieve and ignore.

By the morning of June 5, it was too late. And by that night, men like Fire Department Captain John O'Neill and his crew were left to clean up the mess.

O'Neill stood by himself on the pile of debris as his men stripped off their rescue gear and, sweat-soaked, tried to recover from the backbreaking and mentally draining work of looking for bodies among the tons of brick, concrete and wood, the rubble of what had once been the Thrift Store. O'Neill was a stately man, tall and chiseled. It was late, and he was tired, wiping sweat from his forehead.

"I just wanted to gather my thoughts," he said later, recalling how he stood alone and looked up at the night sky. "We had just gone through . . . not a thing you'd want to go through in life. But that's our job. That's what we do. And you know, we had a job to finish."

After all the noise and the hustle and bustle, he said, there was a "strange quiet" as he stood and looked toward the sky.

"I'm standing there by myself and out of nowhere I hear 'Help.' Very weak, 'Help'!"

The voice, O'Neill said, reminded him of the sounds that come from one of those talking children's dolls that have a string attached to the back. The voice he heard resembled the faded sound of a doll after the cord starts to rewind. O'Neill said he didn't know how to react. He wondered if he was imagining it, if the prolonged hours of rescue work that day had taken a toll.

"I had to gain my thoughts," he said, "to see if I was actually hearing it, or just wishing I was hearing it. And then I heard it again."

O'Neill instantly dropped to his knees, threw off his helmet and started clearing away the rubble under his feet. He saw some movement, some pieces of clothing that weren't Thrift Store sale items, but rather part of a person trapped beneath him.

"We've got a live one!" he screamed as members of his crew scrambled back into action. They worked feverishly. After hours of extrication—of clawing through rubble by hand to recover a dead body—this was a rescue operation again. Someone was alive underneath the debris. And their job was to get that person out.

It's careful work. Once a body has been located, the removal has to be done by hand. You don't want to risk causing a collapse that might drop more concrete, brick or wood onto the victim. O'Neill saw the woman first. She was, he would later say, "in a catcher's crouch" position, hunched down, her knees bent, her back and head leaning forward. By chance, she had been "compressed down into a void," he said. "She was in between two pieces of wood. She had no room to move and I had to hold her there." She had been squatting for thirteen hours straight and could not move a muscle.

As the rescue workers carefully removed the debris around her, she wanted to try to stand up. O'Neill knew that was dangerous, even life-threatening. He called it the "crush syndrome," something he and others in his line of work were schooled in. So his job, as the debris was pulled away, was to make sure the woman didn't move.

"Her waist was basically her tourniquet," O'Neill said. If she stood up, toxins and poisons that had gathered in the bottom half of her body would rush upward and could kill her. The rescue, O'Neill said, was a "choreographed removal." And while it was underway, he began talking to the woman. Her name was Mariya Plekan. She was a fifty-two-year-old Ukrainian immigrant who frequently shopped at the store, looking for clothes and other items she could send back to her family, a sister, aunts, uncles and two grown children in Ukraine. She had been breathing through a small hole in the rubble and calling for help for hours, she said, but had given up. She thought she was going to die. She wanted to know what had happened.

O'Neill tried to keep her calm and keep her from moving. He spoke with her in a quiet tone as his rescue team went about its work. Mariya, whose English was halting at best, could not understand everything he was saying. The language barrier added to her confusion and terror. At one point in the course of their conversation, he called her by the wrong name.

She corrected him.

"And I thought, what a feisty woman this is," O'Neill said, his voice full of emotion and admiration. "She's the first person I've ever had to survive a building collapse. . . . It's a miracle. . . . Thirteen hours. . . . How, how do you do that?"

She became known as the "Miracle on Market Street," but the miracle wasn't one with a happy ending. Mariya Plekan was rushed to a hospital and stabilized, although there were several times when doctors weren't sure she would make it. Thirteen hours under the rubble had taken a terrible toll. The lower half of her body was destroyed. She would eventually undergo what in the medical profession is known as a guillotine amputation. The lower half of her body, from her hips down, was surgically removed.

She has lived through multiple surgeries, scores of infections as well as kidney and respiratory failure. That she is alive today is a tribute to O'Neill and his rescue team and to dozens of doctors and nurses who have provided expert medical treatment and care at the Hospital of the University of Pennsylvania.

My wife, Gwen, and I were driving home from Newark International Airport shortly after the building collapse had occurred. We had just returned from a relaxing ten-day trip to Italy to celebrate our twenty-fifth wedding anniversary. It was the first time we had been to Florence and Venice together, and it was magical—just as we had been told it would be by so many others who helped assist with our daily itinerary. I always believed that one vacation a year with just me and Gwen was necessary. Even though my schedule is always hectic, I feel it's important to just get away from it all.

As we were on our way to our home in the Philadelphia suburbs, I was stunned to hear the reports about the collapse on the car radio. I began to wonder about who was involved, whether anyone I knew might have been in the building, which is just a short ten-block walk from the Kline & Specter Law Offices at 15th and Locust Streets where I practice as a trial lawyer.

Naturally, I also wondered about the legal ramifications of the case and whether I or anyone else in our firm would get involved. Kline &

Specter, P.C. is considered, and rightly so I believe, one of the best personal injury and medical malpractice law firms in the country. At first blush, however, this appeared to be a "construction/demolition" case, not the kind of litigation I'm usually involved with.

But it turned out to be much more than that.

At the time, I had no way of knowing how much that building collapse would monopolize my time and affect my life both professionally and personally. A few days later, I was sitting in my office when the phone rang. A woman was calling on behalf of a close friend who was a victim of the collapse. She asked if I could help.

Her friend was Mariya Plekan.

CHAPTER TWO

MARIYA PLEKAN was rushed by ambulance to the Hospital of the University of Pennsylvania, locally referred to as HUP. In a city blessed with some of the top medical facilities in the country, HUP is considered by many to be one of the best. It also happened to be the closest to the accident scene. As a result, it was where most of the victims were taken.

"Patient was transported lights & sirens to Hospital of the Univ. of PA" read the ambulance record from the Philadelphia Fire Department that night. Using that same type of shorthand, the initial hospital report would describe the patient as a "52 y/o F pulled from rubble of building collapse >12 hrs at site."

A more detailed assessment followed. It was not a pretty picture. Doctors were unsure whether Mariya would survive. And if she did, they knew, things would never be the same for her.

"The patient is critically ill with circulatory failure, renal failure, respiratory failure, hematologic failure, severe metabolic derangement(s) and severe/multiple trauma" read a critical assessment shortly after she arrived. For Mariya Plekan it was the beginning of months of pain and agony, the start of a fight for her life, a fight she would win, but for which she would pay a terrible price.

Investigations into the collapse began almost immediately. Philadelphia Mayor Michael Nutter, being interviewed live on CNN while the rescue operation was underway, said the Fire Department, the City Office of Licenses and Inspections (L&I) and the federal Occupational Safety and Health Administration (OSHA) each would be undertaking its own probe. The goal, said the mayor as he stood in front of the collapsed building, was to determine "what happened, why it happened and whether there's any responsibility to be assigned to whoever was doing the job."

In an ominous note for those who might be criminally liable, two homicide prosecutors from the Philadelphia District Attorney's Office were also on scene.

There was, in fact, more than enough responsibility to go around. But in the immediate aftermath of the tragedy, it became a blame game that focused on just a few people. Why and how the wall collapsed were the threshold questions and led quite naturally to the two men directly involved in the demolition project, Griffin Campbell and Sean Benschop.

Campbell, a broad-shouldered forty-eight-year-old construction contractor, had been hired to take down several buildings along the 2100 and 2200 blocks of Market Street. He was described by those who knew him as hardworking and serious about his business. He had a wife and family and for years had been on the streets scratching out a living. For a time he owned a food truck, and then he was involved in rehabbing and flipping houses. Ultimately, he had set up his own construction company, doing small jobs throughout the city. His previous experience in demolition was limited, two jobs involving the demolition of some abandoned row houses.

The project on Market Street was his first major demolition work. How he was able to obtain a demolition permit would be one of the preliminary questions raised as various agencies began to analyze what had happened.

The simplest answer was that the City had very few regulations when it came to private demolition projects. That would change after the City Council held hearings and adopted stricter building code regulations. In the long run, those changes were a good thing, but they did nothing at that moment for the victims of the collapse. They did, however, highlight the City's potential fault in the disaster.

Campbell was hired by Plato Marinakos Jr., a local architect who had been retained to oversee the demolition of the Market Street buildings. This was to be the first phase of a grandiose plan by the property owner, Richard Basciano, and his company STB Investments. Basciano, who had made a fortune dealing in real estate in midtown Manhattan, hoped to do the same in Philadelphia, where he had extensive property holdings. For several years, he had been promoting what he called a "Gateway to Philadelphia" project that would give a facelift to an aging section of Market Street and link it with the more bustling University City area, several blocks to the west, and to the thriving Center City area, a few blocks to the east.

All the buildings were supposed to be down by April 30, 2013, under the terms of a contract Campbell had signed several months earlier. In the aftermath of what happened, many would take note of the fact that Campbell was by far the low bidder on the job. He proposed doing all the work for $112,000. The next lowest bidder came in at over $300,000. Should that exceptionally low bid have given Marinakos or Basciano any concern about the quality of work? That would be one of the recurring questions as civil litigants lined up to stake claims.

Among other things, Campbell would explain that his low bid was in part due to his plan to salvage the wooden joists and heavy supporting beams in the structures. That, in turn, would lead to a demolition approach that experts would later say was totally wrong for the project.

The building at 2136 Market Street was four stories high. It had once housed a sandwich shop called Hoagie City on the first floor and apartments on the three floors above. Like all the other buildings Campbell was hired to take down, the property was empty. It had been vacant for several years. Because Campbell wanted to salvage everything of value, he began to demolish the building from front to back, removing joists and flooring from inside the property while leaving the walls standing. His approach was based in part on his belief that the Salvation Army would provide reasonable access to the roof of its building to complete the demolition safely. Experts would later testify that the proper way to take the building down was top to bottom. This was especially important because the Hoagie City building, unlike the others along Market Street that Campbell had already demolished, was adjacent to a thriving business—the Salvation Army Thrift Store at 22nd and Market.

Benschop, forty-two, had more experience in the demolition business. A thin, wiry man who had come to the United States from his native Guyana, he estimated that he had demolished about four hundred properties throughout the city, nothing major, but the kind of work that allowed him to claim that he was adept at operating an excavator, a machine slightly larger than a backhoe with a claw that would be used to pull small walls down. A friend had introduced Benschop to Campbell at a Home Depot shortly before the Market Street project began, around February of 2013. Campbell hired Benschop to do some backhoe and excavating work on the other buildings and called him back to the job site after the demolition of the Hoagie City building had stalled.

Benschop was in effect a day contractor. He charged Campbell $800 a day "for me and the excavator." He had done work clearing debris at both the 2100 and 2200 Market Street sites and had left the job on May 15th with the hollowed hulk of the Hoagie City building still standing.

By that point, Campbell was two weeks behind schedule. Basciano, whose STB Investments was the titular owner of the project, had come by the site a few times and had asked Marinakos, the architect, what was taking so long and why the building wasn't down. Campbell knew about Basciano's concerns, and he also had some vague information about a problem with the Salvation Army's permitting access to the roof of its store. In fact, Basciano's people and representatives of the Salvation Army had been going back and forth for nearly two months about the project. Neither side appeared to be listening to the other. The Salvation Army ignored warnings about possible danger when Basciano's representatives requested access and seemed more concerned about potential property damage than the safety of its employees and customers. Basciano's people grew frustrated and at one point talked about creating a situation that would require L&I to intervene and cite the Salvation Army for creating a hazard. Neither side seemed to trust the other.

More details about just how cavalier and indifferent both sides appeared and about how greed and the bottom line seemed to be driving the controversy would surface as investigations and civil litigation moved forward. But Griffin Campbell and Sean Benschop were the men left holding the bag.

Campbell wanted access to the roof of the Thrift Store, and had that been granted, he might have been able to push the unstable wall into the collapsed interior of the Hoagie City building. In fact, when Benschop was called back to the site in June a few days before the wall collapsed, that's what he and Campbell discussed.

At first, Benschop said, he offered to take down the Hoagie City building himself. He said he wanted $80,000. Campbell, who had bid the whole job for $112,000, couldn't go for that. Then Benschop proposed taking the wall down "brick by brick." His price, $11,000 per floor. His idea was to bring an aerial lift in, set it up on 22nd Street and work over the top of the Thrift Store roof.

Two men in a bucket, he said, would take the wall down by hand. They'd do the work at night using hand tools, sledgehammers, wrecking bars and an impact gun, which he described as a small, handheld jackhammer. The work would be slow and tedious. But the job would get done. He thought two two-men crews, alternating in the bucket every hour or so, would be able to finish the job safely. And because they'd be working at night, the demolition would take place while the store was closed.

Again, Campbell rejected the idea.

On June 2, 2013, Benschop, using his excavator, began some cleanup work around the Hoagie City site. On June 3, a Monday, it rained. No work was done. On June 4, Benschop began ripping down the Hoagie City storefront, largely exposing the gutted interior of the building, which at that point included a back wall and the two side walls, each about four stories high. Most of the supporting joists that held the walls up were gone. Benschop was due back the next day to continue working the excavator.

He woke up around 5 a.m. on June 5, 2013, and did what he said he had been doing every morning for nearly a dozen years. He smoked a joint. Marijuana, he said, was part of his daily routine. He had a medical condition that caused him to lose his appetite, but marijuana made him hungry. For a time, he claimed, he'd had a doctor's prescription for medication that enhanced his appetite. But his insurance had run out and he could no longer afford to buy the pills.

Weed was cheaper.

He smoked every morning and every evening.

When he arrived at the site on June 5, around 9 a.m., he had had his breakfast and was ready for work. He waited for Campbell, who was bringing fuel for the excavator. Benschop's job that day was to take down the eastern wall of the Hoagie City building, the wall farthest away from the Thrift Store. He had a small steel beam, salvaged from the work site, in the claws of the excavator and would use it to knock small sections of the brick wall into the collapsed interior of the Hoagie City site. He called it "peeling" the wall. He started around the third floor.

"I take the beam and I start poking the wall," he later explained.

While he worked, he said, he noticed that Campbell was talking to a well-dressed older man and woman who had arrived at the site. Benschop would claim these people had shown up in a white Mercedes. The couple, Richard Basciano and his wife, said they arrived by taxi. It was one of several conflicting stories that emerged.

As Benschop poked at the wall, there was a whooshing sound. He looked up and saw that the far side wall, the wall adjacent to the Thrift Store, was gone.

"The building just collapsed," he said. By chance, a camera from a passing city bus captured the catastrophe in real time on video. It looked like a massive dust storm triggered by a terrorist bomb.

Benschop jumped out of the excavator and stumbled into a hole, falling down and injuring his hand. He scrambled up and found Campbell. The two men looked at one another, and then Benschop asked the question that would haunt all those involved in the project and the all victims who later sought monetary compensation.

"Do you have insurance?' he asked.

Benschop said he and Campbell rushed to the Salvation Army site and tried to help. Rescue crews arrived within minutes, and because of his injured hand, Benschop was taken to a hospital. Blood work would show marijuana and Percocet in his system. Within two days, the District Attorney's Office would issue an arrest warrant.

On June 8, Benschop turned himself in to the authorities, who had charged him with multiple counts of involuntary manslaughter. The District Attorney argued that the amount of marijuana in his system impaired his ability to operate heavy equipment.

The blame game had begun. Mayor Nutter issued a statement after the arrest that clearly indicated where the City believed responsibility lay.

"Sean Benschop finally turned himself in to authorities today," Nutter said. "It is because of his reckless and irresponsible behavior that six people died and thirteen people were hurt and buried under debris and bricks.

"It is my hope that the harshest level of charges are brought against Sean Benschop, and he is punished accordingly. We must also seek answers from property owners Richard Basciano and Griffin T. Campbell who hired Benschop to do the significant job of operating heavy equipment. These three individuals bear the ultimate and sole responsibility for this tragedy. Justice will only be served if Sean Benschop receives a sentence that buries him in a jailhouse forever, just like his victims were buried on Wednesday."

Nutter's rhetoric set the tone. His error about who owned the property—Campbell was merely a contractor—was just one of several inaccurate comments that would emerge from City Hall in the days that followed.

Other news reports provided more details and hinted at problems.

Newspaper and television stories noted that Benschop was also known as Kary Roberts and that since 1994 he had been arrested eleven times. The charges included drug possession, theft and weapons offenses. Benschop had served time in prison for drug trafficking. His last arrest was in January 2012, according to news reports, for aggravated assault. Those charges were dismissed for lack of evidence.

Benschop's lawyer insisted that his client was not impaired while working the demolition job and that what had happened was a terrible accident, but not a crime. Like so much else about the tragedy, that issue would be open to debate and litigation.

News reports also pointed out that neither Philadelphia nor Pennsylvania required demolition contractors to be licensed. And one City official noted that the City code did not require demolition contractors to show any proficiency before being granted a demolition permit.

In fact, in this case it was the architect, Plato Marinakos Jr., who had applied for the permit on Griffin Campbell's behalf.

Nutter, perhaps sensing that the City might share some of the responsibility and blame, was quick to point out that "Buildings get demolished all the time in the city of Philadelphia with active buildings right next to them. . . . They're done safely in this city all the time. . . . Something obviously went wrong here yesterday and possibly in the days leading up to it. That's what the investigation is for."

The mayor also said he was unaware of any complaints about the demolition work. However, officials at OSHA said a complaint had been filed on May 15 about work at the site. And City officials would later acknowledge that a 311 call (to the City complaint line) on May 15 also raised questions about how the demolition was being conducted and whether proper safety precautions were being taken for pedestrians walking along Market Street.

Questions about the City's response would lead to another tragedy.

On June 12, one week after the collapse, police found Ronald Wagenhoffer dead in his pickup truck parked in the Roxborough section of the city near his home.

Wagenhoffer, fifty-two, had been shot once in the chest. Authorities said the wound was self-inflicted. A City employee for sixteen years, he was the L&I inspector responsible for overseeing the Market Street demolition project. How often he had visited the site would become an issue, but what was certain is that in response to the May 15 complaint, he had driven to the vicinity of that location.

In a video left after his suicide, according to a news report by NBC10, the Philadelphia television station that broke the story, Wagenhoffer said, "It was my fault. I should have looked at those guys working and I didn't. . . . I should have parked my truck and went over there, but I didn't. I'm sorry."

Wagenhoffer's body was discovered by his wife, who had gone looking for him after receiving a text message from him that night. He was said to be distraught over what had happened. His body was discovered at 9:30 p.m.

City officials, in a move that could be described either as coming to his defense or possibly as covering their own backs, disputed the video. Mayor Nutter said that Wagenhoffer had said, "It *wasn't* my fault." The TV station stood by its report.

Another City official told reporters, "This man did nothing wrong. The department did what it was supposed to do under code that existed at the time."

Many people did many things wrong in the lead-up to the collapse that day on Market Street. Wagenhoffer may have been one of them. He would be one of the few who, tragically, accepted responsibility.

Philadelphia City Council would open hearings into the building collapse in August. At the same time the District Attorney, Seth Williams, was conducting a grand jury investigation to see if anyone other than Benschop was criminally liable.

Griffin Campbell was the obvious target; Mayor Nutter had said as much. And the architect, Plato Marinakos Jr., who had hired Campbell and who was charged with overseeing the work, would also come under scrutiny.

Marinakos, however, was given a way out. Shortly after the wall fell, he contacted a lawyer. While the grand jury was investigating, he negotiated a deal. In exchange for immunity from prosecution, he would cooperate with investigators.

Different people deal differently with tragedy, adversity and guilt. Ronald Wagenhoffer never thought he was entitled to immunity.

CHAPTER THREE

O F ALL THE *what ifs* that surfaced after the tragedy—and there were dozens—the one that said the most about the key players was this: What if the Salvation Army had taken Richard Basciano up on his offer to trade a property two blocks away on Market Street for the Thrift Store building? The offer came before demolition even began. If the Salvation Army had taken the deal, then the Thrift Store on June 5 would have been a vacant property, just like the Hoagie City building.

But the Salvation Army never accepted the offer.

Negotiations apparently bogged down late in 2012. In November of that year, in an internal Salvation Army memo, Colonel Timothy Raines, the number two man at regional headquarters in West Nyack, New York, said Basciano and his people were impossible to deal with.

"These people are not serious," Raines wrote, "and have no credibility. They wouldn't know the truth if it slapped them in the face."

Basciano had a different take on the proposal. He claimed he had offered the Salvation Army a generous deal. He said the property he was offering at 2324 Market Street later sold for more than $1 million, much more than the value of the Thrift Store at 2140 Market.

Why the deal fell apart is a question with various answers, depending on who is being asked. But it may have been that the problem—and this gets to the heart of an even broader issue—wasn't the deal. Maybe the problem was Richard Basciano.

Basciano, who had been born and raised in Baltimore and had served his country in the Navy in World War II, went to New York to make his fortune. He found it on 42nd Street, where in the 1970s his property holdings included sex shops, X-rated movie theaters and "adult entertainment centers." One of his biggest was Show World, just off the corner of 42nd and 8th Avenue in the heart of what was then Manhattan's sexually explicit commercial district.

There were an estimated 150 "adult" establishments operating in the area. Basciano and his partners controlled many of them. He was a major figure in the industry. The *New York Times* referred to him as the "Times Square Pornography Magnate" and the "Sultan of Smut." In the *New York Post* he was the "Porn King."

His partners, according to media reports, included Robert "DiB" DiBernardo, a mobster who was linked to the Gambino crime family and who, according to some reports, generated $250 million a year in income for himself and his mob family through pornography, prostitution and labor racketeering.

DiBernardo was an entrepreneurial gangster who eschewed violence. He was what they call "an earner," and he was big-time. Like Basciano, he didn't call attention to himself and preferred to work in the shadows. DiBernardo "disappeared" in 1986. He was last seen driving away from his business in a white Mercedes. Testimony at the trial of Gambino crime family boss John Gotti in 1992 indicated that DiB had been killed by Gotti's underboss, Salvatore "Sammy the Bull" Gravano. The motive was money—or, more precisely, an underworld dispute over money.

Basciano, a former boxer, once protested that he had no idea DiBernardo was a mobster. Given the nature of their business and the mob's control of large swatches of the porn industry nationwide at the time, that's hard to believe. After DiB's demise, Basciano remained a major player in the industry.

Show World, the porn emporium that he had opened in the mid-1970s, was described in the *Times* as a "sleek, 22,000 square foot pornographic supermarket." The paper went on to report that "Basciano made millions of dollars from the quarters that his customers deposited for peep shows and more interactive forms of activity." The gaudy Show World marquee boasted "Adult XXX movies," "Live Nude Girls" and "Hottest Live Acts in US."

The *New York Post*, in a story that focused on 42nd Street's infamous past, called Show World a "glitzy, hard core porn palace . . . a 24/7 carnival of the damned [that] featured naked girls, couples simulating copulation onstage and triple-x rated fare to sate every desire."

Often sporting a tan, his silver-white hair neatly coifed, the always impeccably dressed Basciano was said to live in a penthouse in the twelve-story office/apartment building whose ground floor housed Show World. His penthouse included a full-sized boxing ring.

In the 1990s, with New York cracking down on pornography and with developers looking to gentrify Times Square, Basciano shifted his real estate attention to Philadelphia, where he began to buy up real estate along Market Street. By that point he had sold off most of his Times Square holdings, reaping substantial profits as the neighborhood went upscale and tourists came looking for Disney rather than Deep Throat.

Basciano would hold on to Show World, but it was a decidedly less risqué operation.

In Philadelphia his new holdings included The Forum, one of the last adult movie theaters in the city, as well as a string of adult bookstores that featured peep shows and sex paraphernalia. The Forum was located in the 2200 block of Market Street and was one of the Basciano-controlled buildings demolished before work began on the Hoagie City building one block east.

Not surprisingly, Basciano's curriculum vitae was at odds with the tenets and principles of the Salvation Army. You have to wonder if this difference colored their business relationship. While the point is never spoken and not relevant to the demolition, it's conceivable that the officers from the Salvation Army were less than eager to do business with someone who had made a fortune in the sex industry.

Founded in England in 1865 by a Methodist Reform Church minister named William Booth, the Salvation Army was built around the three S's—soup, soap and salvation. Sex was an activity limited to the bedroom and to heterosexual couples who were married. Described as a quasi-military charitable organization, the "Army" quickly took its mission worldwide. Today it boasts more than 1.5 million members. The public's most common reference might be the red kettles that pop up at Christmas staffed by jovial volunteers ringing handheld bells as they solicit donations. But that folksy image belies an institutional behemoth. Operating in 127 countries, the Salvation Army in 2013 publicly reported total revenues of more than $4 billion, expenses in excess of $3 billion and total net assets of $10.7 billion. Today, its net worth is even *higher*, and information relating to its impressive fortune is publicly available.

Those assets were equal to or greater than those of some major Fortune 500 companies. Nike, for example, had net assets of $10.7 billion, the same as the Salvation Army. Assets of the Hilton hotel chain and related companies were a little more than $9 billion. Amazon came in at slightly over $7 billion. Starbucks and Best Buy were paltry in comparison. Each had total net assets of slightly more than $3 billion.

Financially, the Salvation Army was a major-league operation that had succeeded at keeping its overwhelming affluence under the radar. In the world of charity giving, it was also top-rated. Watchdog groups who track that industry consistently award the Salvation Army a grade of A or A– for its financial efficiency and transparency. But its tradition was steeped in old-fashioned fire and brimstone, the kind of preaching and proselytizing that would have targeted Basciano as a sinner in need of salvation. Its symbolic crest is emblazoned with the slogan "Blood and Fire." The motto is explained in Salvation Army literature: "Jesus' blood washes us clean. Fire of Holy Spirit purifies us."

Simply put, then, the Salvation Army and Richard Basciano were not a good fit.

This was *Guys and Dolls* with an edge. For years, the charitable organization had taken a strong moral stand against pornography. In 2014, it memorialized that stand in a position paper that read in part: "Pornography attacks and distorts God's purpose for human relationships . . . depersonalizes sexuality, emphasizing the carnal to the neglect of loving relationships and commitment. Instead of providing intimacy, pornography only intensifies lust based on fantasy."

Basciano clearly had a different view, once telling a reporter that his business helped discourage and reduce the incidents of rape.

None of this, of course, had anything to do with the building collapse on June 5, 2013.

Or did it?

The attitudes and backgrounds of the players may help explain the actions—or lack thereof—that led up to the disaster that day. Problems apparently had started at least a year earlier when, Basciano said, he tried to negotiate the property swap with the Salvation Army.

"I was surprised that they made a very stupid decision," Basciano said later. "If they had taken the generous offer it [the wall collapse] would have been superfluous. We would have owned the property and this never would have happened."

Instead, in the spring of 2013, Basciano's organization, STB Investments, began discussions with the Salvation Army about the Hoagie City demolition project and its potential impact on the Thrift Store.

Perhaps "discussions" is not the right word. Emails and letters that would become part of voluminous civil litigation seem to demonstrate that the two sides were talking at one another rather than with one another; that each side quickly staked out a position and was unwilling to budge. "Listening" focused on formulating a reply—not attempting to understand the underlying safety issues.

Thomas Simmonds Jr., a property manager for Basciano, was the point man in most of the correspondence, along with Joel Oshtry, one of Basciano's lawyers. Plato Marinakos, the architect who had hired Griffin Campbell, also weighed in from time to time. For the Army, there was Colonel Raines, Major Charles Deitrick, Major John Cranford, a property manager named Alistair Fraser and lawyer Stephen Nudel. Fraser was charged with overseeing the operation of 280 thrift stores in the Salvation Army's eastern region. Cranford was an administrator whose responsibilities included overseeing thrift store operations, including the store at 2140 Market Street.

Deitrick and Cranford would eventually emerge as key players. But it was an email from Salvation Army attorney Stephen Nudel, written a day before the building collapsed, that underscored one of the principal arguments I would make in the civil trial that defined the tragedy. The point was that no one involved cared about safety or about protecting the lives of those who worked and shopped in the store.

Nudel's email on June 4, 2013, was in response to a series of emails that had been going back and forth for weeks. Among other things, Basciano's organization was trying to get access to the roof of the Thrift Store to safely demolish the adjacent building.

An earlier email suggested that the Basciano organization wanted to place a truck with a boom on 22nd Street and use the boom lift over the roof in order to knock down the wall. This was in many ways similar to Benschop's aerial lift and two-men-in-a-bucket solution. But for reasons that never were made clear, the Basciano group did not follow up on its own proposal.

Cost may have been the reason.

The correspondence in the weeks leading up to the collapse indicated that the Salvation Army offered less than clear answers to the questions, pleadings and warnings of the Basciano group and often appeared more concerned with protecting its investment than with ensuring the safety of its workers and customers.

Nudel's email, written less than twenty-four hours before the wall came down, reiterated concerns that the Salvation Army had raised in earlier emails and ended by asking the Basciano organization to "please advise what procedures will be implemented to minimize vibrations within the Salvation Army premises. There's a concern that your work will cause damage to our display items."

That, to me, said it all.

A day before six people were killed and a seventh was buried alive for thirteen hours, the Salvation Army—one of the preeminent charitable organizations in the world and a company with more than $10 billion in assets—was more concerned with possible damage to secondhand display items than with the safety of those for whom it was responsible.

This position formed the spine around which the civil suit on behalf of Mariya Plekan and the other plaintiffs would be built. It would be more than three years before a jury would get to consider that point, but early on it was what drove our litigation.

The email record leading up to June 5, 2013, is replete with other examples of intransigence and indifference. Even more troubling is the fact that City officials were copied on many of those emails and chose to either disregard or ignore them. One City official later said he never read the emails, claiming they were sent to an address that he seldom used.

What is clear from a reading of those documents and from the positions taken by the major players is that this tragedy should have been avoided.

The first "warning" from STB to the Salvation Army went out on February 5, 2013, when Marinakos, after a field survey of sorts on the state of buildings in the 2100 block, wrote to the Salvation Army that the Thrift Store building was in terrible shape.

"Based on a field inspection and our engineering judgment, it is our conclusion that the structural condition of subject building is barely sound and in extreme state of neglect and disrepair," Marinakos wrote.

The Salvation Army responded by sending a masonry, paint and wallpaper company representative to check out the store. Not a structural engineer. Not an architect. His report two days later indicated that there was some water damage on the first floor and basement, but he attributed it to "water infiltrating the adjoining property." The adjoining property was the four-story vacant apartment building with the Hoagie City storefront.

Demolition work began a short time later. Workers in the Thrift Store would complain to one another about the noise, the vibrations that shook the party wall the store shared with the Hoagie City property, and the debris that was falling inside the wall and occasionally sending clouds of dust into the store.

"My God, it's going to fall," store manager Margarita Agosto said she told a Salvation Army field supervisor named Ralph Pomponi, who had visited the store while demolition was going full tilt. "Don't worry about it," she said he told her. "Nothing is going to happen."

Richard Stasiorowski, the assistant store manager, said the rumblings became the source of gallows humor for the employees in the weeks leading up to the collapse. He said that he, Agosto and others would nervously "joke" about the constant chaos and the dust and debris. There would be guarded laughter whenever anyone mentioned a possible collapse.

"It's something that you never think is going to happen, but it was something that we did discuss amongst ourselves," said Stasiorowski, who also acknowledged that the condition of the Thrift Store building even before the demolition work began was deplorable.

Part of the ceiling was cracked and falling in one part of the store, and the basement, where men's clothing was on display and sorting sometimes took place, was a "dungeon" populated by rats, he said.

Relatively speaking, he and Agosto were lucky. They managed to get out of the building on June 5. Several of their co-workers did not. More important, *none*—not Agosto, not Stasiorowski, not any of the other employees—were told of the emails between STB and the Salvation Army and the growing safety concerns being expressed by Simmonds, Basciano's New York–based property manager. The employees of the Salvation Army were left in the dark.

Colonel Raines and others would later say there was "no need" to inform the workers and customers of the issues being discussed in those emails. It appeared that he and Major Cranford had decided that warnings were a ploy by STB to get the Salvation Army either to reconsider a property swap or to allow demolition workers to have access to the roof of the Thrift Store.

Notes from a Salvation Army production meeting that February indicate that Cranford and the others were prepared to do legal battle after Marinakos's initial email raising questions about the building's structure and after the Salvation Army got indications that STB might ask the City and its office of Licenses and Inspections to intervene.

The Salvation Army saw this tactic as STB's "playing hardball." Throughout the months leading up to the tragedy, the Salvation Army's take on the situation was economic.

"Major [Cranford] said this will probably be settled in courts," the memo from that February 13 production meeting read in part. "He said loosing [i.e., losing] this store would loose [lose] a lot of money for the Center and it is number one in top quality donations. Major said the structure of the building remains sound, and we must show that proof to the city because of accusations that the building was not sound."

By May 2013 the last phase of the demolition work was underway. Griffin Campbell was effectively gutting the Hoagie City building. Simmonds sent a second email to Salvation Army officials complaining about their failure to respond to earlier inquiries and detailing two important issues: the status of the Thrift Store chimney, if and when the Hoagie City wall was taken down, and the need for Campbell to gain access to the Thrift Store roof. STB, he said, wanted to temporarily install safety devices—tarp and other equipment—"to prevent any accidents and damage to your property."

The next day a conference call between the parties led to a belief on the part of Basciano's people that an agreement was going to be worked out for roof access. The Salvation Army would contend that the phone call was merely a discussion and that an agreement, if it came, would be the result of more talks. That position seemed to be at odds with an STB summary of the meeting, which noted that "the parties will agree to work on a collaborative and neighborly basis to expedite the completion of a smooth demolition process."

Major Deitrick, in a May 10 email, had a different take on the situation, indicating that the Salvation Army would work through its "professionals"—a lawyer and an architect—to "meet our neighborly goals but at the same time *protect our own investment.* As stated, no commitments are made at this point . . ." (emphasis added).

Deitrick, as most Salvation Army officials did, signed off with "Thank you. Have Blessed Day."

Blessed would not be the word that came to mind in analyzing these "negotiations" after the fact. Among other things, the Salvation Army said it believed all demolition would be stopped until an agreement was reached.

STB said no such understanding existed.

And if the Salvation Army officials had bothered to check with anyone in the doomed Thrift Store, they would have learned that Campbell and Benschop were continuing to claw away at what was becoming a dangerous and unstable Hoagie City property.

"Every minute that passes increases the liability of all parties," Simmonds wrote in May in response to questions raised by Fraser, the Salvation Army property manager, who was asking who had responsibility for making sure the Thrift Store building remained water-tight and maintained its "structural integrity" as the demolition was completed. What's more, Fraser wanted to know who would be responsible for fixing any cracks in the interior walls and ceiling after the demolition was over.

Once the collapse occurred, of course, cracks in the ceiling were no longer an issue, but the subject and tenor of the Salvation Army's emails underscore the cavalier attitude that the charitable organization displayed in the run-up to the tragedy.

In the aftermath, Colonel Raines and Major Cranford both said they did not take the warnings from Simmonds or Marinakos seriously, calling the warnings "hyperbole." "Same old same old," Cranford said of the concerns that were being raised in a more urgent manner as the demolition moved forward.

On May 13, Simmonds urged the Salvation Army to respond to the request for roof access, warning that "your response is required to avoid potential damage to the subject properties as well as the public." He then said that STB might go to court and "seek injunctive relief" if the Salvation Army failed to respond.

In retrospect, had Simmonds acted on that threat, had STB gone to court, the City might have been forced to intervene and at least temporarily shut the project down. Instead, the war of words continued.

On May 15, Joel Oshtry, an STB lawyer, wrote a letter to Nudel, the Salvation Army attorney, warning that "it is now a matter of urgency that this demolition be accomplished immediately. The [Hoagie City] building . . . is in a state of partial demolition . . . the longer it remains undemolished the greater the risks to the public and all property owners of an uncontrolled collapse." That same day, Simmonds sent a prophetic email to the Salvation Army officials, stating that "continued delays in responding pose a threat to life, limb and public safety." A week later, on May 22, he emailed City officials repeating his concerns and warning about "those headlines none of us wants to read."

Two City officials appeared to be copied on that email. Neither responded.

The Salvation Army continued to drag its feet. In an internal email, Nudel, the lawyer, urged Majors Deitrick and Cranford to "*not* enter into a separate agreement with the property owner [STB] and simply direct them to comply with code" (emphasis added).

At the same time, Nudel sent a letter to Oshtry, STB's lawyer, in which he reiterated the concerns he had raised about potential structural damage that the demolition might cause to the Thrift Store, ending with, "Finally, since my client intends to remain open and operating, invitees [customers] and personnel will need to be protected. Access will need to be coordinated with Major Cranford to ensure your timing has a minimal disruption to our business."

Despite Nudel's assertion, Cranford apparently had no intention of giving STB access to the roof of the Thrift Store. At a production meeting on May 22, Cranford's wife, Karen, also a Salvation Army major, had raised safety concerns and wondered if the store, its workers and its content could be temporarily relocated until the demolition was over. Hers was one of the few sensible suggestions to surface in the pile of memos, emails and other correspondence that tracked what was going on internally in the months leading up to the tragedy. Major Cranford basically sidestepped his wife's concerns, telling her that possible relocation of the store was a hurdle that would be faced at a later date. This chauvinist attitude closely corresponded with the fact that when Major John Cranford and Major Karen Cranford were in the same room together, Major Karen Cranford would be referred to as "Mrs. Major."

In addition, according to a Salvation Army dispatcher who attended those production meetings, Cranford was adamant about not letting STB onto the Thrift Store property. "In his opinion, they had no business being on his roof," said Edward Strudwick. "Everything was his. It was his roof, his playground, you're not coming on it."

Strudwick, who would later testify at the civil trial, said no one would speak up once Cranford took a position. "It was his way or no way," he said. "I felt concerned, but you never spoke back to Major Cranford. That was your first step out the door."

Plato Marinakos, who in many ways had set the tragic process in motion, tried desperately in the days leading up to the collapse to control or contain the situation. On June 2, he proposed a partial demolition of the unstable wall, leaving part of it supporting the Thrift Store chimney. At that point, he suggested, STB could notify City officials of a dangerous situation and put the onus on the Salvation Army, since it was the Army's chimney. By June 4, after examining the gutted Hoagie City building with its unstable and unsupported walls, he told Griffin Campbell to do something immediately. They talked of erecting scaffolding on the Hoagie City side of the wall and taking down the wall by hand.

But that proposal was ludicrous on its face. There was no way four stories of scaffolding could be erected in a short period of time. What's more, there was nowhere to base the scaffolding. The interior of the Hoagie City building was an uneven pile of brick and debris, not level ground on which scaffolding could be mounted. And there was nowhere to anchor the scaffolding even if it could be erected.

Marinakos said Campbell promised him he would have a crew work through the night of June 4 into June 5 to get the wall down. It never happened. By that point, it may have been too late.

Marinakos could not get STB, the company he worked for, or the Salvation Army to focus on the danger he saw at the demolition site. His failure to oversee the project properly and his inability to get anyone to fix the problem posed by the unsupported wall point to his responsibility and accountability for what happened. But responsibility and accountability, from my perspective, went far beyond the architect.

"You had two competing interests here," he would later say. "You had STB on the one side and you had Salvation Army on the other side. And they wouldn't listen to each other."

Maybe the Salvation Army officials never intended to listen.

Maybe Richard Basciano was just someone with whom they did not want to do business. Maybe it was a moral decision colored by economics and made at the expense of the safety of their customers and employees.

The Mayor's Office, City Council, the District Attorney and OSHA would all launch investigations into the collapse. The media, local and national, continued to report on the tragedy. The story line from the very beginning was that incompetent and poorly planned demolition was the cause of what had happened.

Several plaintiff attorneys, including Robert Mongeluzzi, quickly adopted that position as well. His stance, and a photo of him wearing a hard hat at the scene, were included in a front-page *Philadelphia Inquirer* article on June 10, 2013, five days after the collapse. Mongeluzzi had a lot of experience in construction accident litigation. It's what he knows and what he is good at. But from my perspective, this was *much* more than a construction accident.

Mongeluzzi was also the first lawyer to file a lawsuit on behalf of a client in the case, and this fact would later be used as leverage for decision making when there were disagreements during the trial. The applicable rules of procedure suggest that the party who files the first lawsuit may present his case first. Mongeluzzi voiced his intention to exercise that option, and we had to work through that issue. Ironically, though he did file his lawsuit first, he did not sue the Salvation Army. He sued only Richard Basciano, STB Investments Corp., Griffin T. Campbell, and Campbell's company, Nicetown House Development Corporation—the demolition defendants.

In my view, the demolition question was a piece, but a relatively small piece, of a bigger problem. Six people died, and Mariya Plekan was buried alive for thirteen hours, her life and limbs destroyed in the process. She was the most catastrophically injured survivor. She would need care, extremely expensive care, for the rest of her life. It would be easy to join the crowd and fix blame on Campbell and Benschop, and by extension Marinakos and Basciano. But that would do nothing for Mariya and other victims, nor would it address what I felt was the key issue in the case.

My position, from day one, was that this tragedy was rooted in the indifference, mistrust and arrogance of the Salvation Army. And from the beginning to the end of this tragic story, that never changed.

About a week after Mongeluzzi had focused blame on the incompetent construction-related parties, I was also interviewed by the news media. I made it clear that not just the contractor and the excavator operator were at fault; I said there were many potentially responsible parties to blame. I wanted to keep the Salvation Army and others in the crosshairs. In part, I had to keep matters purposely ambiguous in light of the comments made by Mongeluzzi and others that fixated on the incompetent demolition. I said I planned to sue "several people." Of Mariya, I said: "She's paid a heavy price—half her body was removed.

But when I get done, all the people responsible are going to pay, because this shouldn't have happened."

"There's going to be a lot of people and corporations trying to deny responsibility and avoid their responsibility, and we're not going to let that happen," I said. "Let the games begin . . ."

CHAPTER FOUR

I FIRST MET Mariya Plekan in the intensive care unit at the Hospital of the University of Pennsylvania on June 16, 2013, eleven days after the collapse. It's a day I will never forget. Dariya Tareb, who was Mariya's friend and the person who had contacted me about possibly representing her, was there along with Mariya's two adult children, Natalia and Andrii, who had recently arrived from Ukraine. The University Hospital physicians were invaluable in explaining what Mariya had already endured.

After Mariya was rushed by ambulance to HUP, the medical priorities that night were to stabilize her condition and try to salvage her legs. The surgeons had initially performed what is known as bilateral fasciotomies. That is, they cut the connective tissues below her skin to relieve tremendous pressure secondary to her extensive crush injuries. This approach didn't work. Within a short time, they had to perform *guillotine* amputations above both knees. A guillotine amputation involves surgical removal of limbs because of extensive trauma and infection. The skin and bone are severed at the same level and the wound is left open for further management. Historically, these amputations were commonplace with soldiers on a battlefield. They are life-altering but, in the best of a worst-case scenario, they can be life-saving procedures. That was the case with Mariya.

To gain admittance to the intensive care unit, all visitors were required to wear sterile protective gowns and face masks. Mariya's brightly lit room, which had a distinct antiseptic smell, contained a bewildering array of intricate medical monitoring devices and life-sustaining equipment. Dariya served as translator and was extremely helpful during that first visit and in dozens of visits that would follow. But she, along with Mariya's children, understandably welled up as they struggled to convey background information. I was mesmerized by the relatively stoic manner in which Mariya was handling her dreadful situation. Her eyes were focused and steady, and she showed little emotion as she nodded and shook her head at appropriate times in response to questions.

It's hard to imagine how anyone would be able to deal with the trauma and tragedy that had befallen her. And while she certainly had her moments of despair, she consistently demonstrated grace under pressure and stoicism in the face of adversity.

She was and remains to this day one of the most remarkable people I have ever met.

Mariya was born in a small town in western Ukraine near the city of Lviv. She was the oldest of five children. Her mother and father were farmers, scratching to earn a living and support their family. She wanted to be a nurse but never had the opportunity. Instead, she worked in a factory and went to a technical school, where she took culinary courses and studied to be a nurse's assistant. She eventually got a job as a cook in a medical school, working in the cafeteria that served students and teachers.

Her husband, Romano Romanovich, was a factory worker. After they married, they lived with his family. He died of lung cancer, leaving her with two children to care for. Andrii was nine at the time. Natalia was eight.

Her family and her husband's family helped, but it was a struggle to survive. Life, she said, was "difficult."

Mariya, I quickly learned, was not one to complain about her circumstances. She was a fighter and devoted to her children.

"In Ukraine, not that easy to live," she said through an interpreter. "No jobs. Money was our biggest problem." And when the Soviet Union collapsed, she said, things got even worse.

For that reason, in 2002, she made the difficult decision to come to the United States to care for her husband's married aunt, who was in poor health and living in Philadelphia.

"She was like a second mother to us," she would say later of the aunt.

She left her children, then teenagers, in the care of her sister and regularly sent cash, clothes (usually purchased at a Salvation Army Thrift Store) and other goods to her family back in Ukraine. Having obtained a green card, she stayed in Philadelphia after both her husband's aunt and the aunt's elderly husband died. It wasn't something she had planned to do. She never thought her stay would be permanent, but the financial opportunities here and the ability to help her children and family back in Ukraine made the choice easier. She would travel back to visit on occasion, but she said she realized she could do more for her children by working in Philadelphia.

"What I do, I do for my children," she said. "I am a mother and I have to care for them."

At the time of the building collapse, Mariya was a caretaker for another elderly Ukrainian woman and had become a part of the Ukrainian-American community in Philadelphia, attending the Church of St. Nicholas at 24th and Poplar and participating in church and neighborhood activities.

She lived in a row house in the Hunting Park section of North Philadelphia. It was a poor neighborhood, and she was clearly an outsider; the community is predominantly Hispanic and African American. But she said older residents looked out for her and made her feel welcome.

"Philadelphia is beautiful," she told me. "History. Culture. And the people are good to me. I didn't live in the nicest neighborhood, but compared to Ukraine, it was nice."

All the while, she was sending money and other goods back to her children, both of whom were able to obtain university degrees in part because of her financial support. Her daughter became a pharmacist. Her son worked in business management.

In today's political climate, in which immigration and immigrants are unfortunately stereotyped and belittled by some, Mariya Plekan was an example of what the inscription on the Statue of Liberty has long symbolized—the "American dream." She had come to America looking for a better life, for an opportunity to succeed. And she had found it and had worked very hard to maintain it.

It is not without irony that two other victims of the June 5, 2013, tragedy were part of that same story. Borbor Davis, a Salvation Army worker who was trapped in the basement and died in the rubble, came from Liberia. Roseline Conteh, a nurse's aide shopping in the store that morning, was from Sierra Leone. Conteh came to the United States in 2003 after being selected in one of those diversity visa lotteries that the current administration finds appalling. She was given an opportunity and made the best of it, bringing three of her four children to this country and working on getting the fourth here.

Mariya Plekan took the Number Seven bus run by SEPTA, the local transit authority, from her home to the Salvation Army Thrift Store that morning. She had a four-hour window of free time and wanted to do some shopping. She was looking for some things she could send back to relatives.

It was a warm, sunny spring morning. If she hadn't needed to shop, it was likely she would have taken a walk. She loved to stroll her adopted city and visit Philadelphia museums, parks and historic sites, where she would take photographs to send back to her children.

The Art Museum area was one of her favorite spots. "It's so beautiful there," she said.

But on that Wednesday, the Thrift Store was her destination.

"It's a little cheaper than the regular stores," she said, offering an explanation that was common to many who shopped there. "I needed to buy something for myself and my relatives, and I had to save money on things."

She noticed nothing unusual when she stepped off the bus at 22nd and Market Streets and headed for the store. From the location where she entered the store, she could not view the ongoing demolition next door.

"I was looking at the . . . signs on the doors for the specials that they have for the day," she said.

There already were people in the store, shoppers and Salvation Army employees dressed in blue smocks. She headed down one of the aisles in the middle of the store, looking at clothing, sorting through for possible buys.

Within minutes her life changed forever.

"I was looking through the clothes and all of a sudden I heard the noise," she would later say. "I had a chance to turn around and look and the roof went down. And the only thing that I had a chance to say is why and the roof collapsed. And it pinned me down, my legs."

Each time she told the story—and she would tell it several times over the course of the investigation and criminal and civil litigation—Mariya Plekan never wavered. She was clearly in pain both physically and mentally, but she wanted—perhaps needed—to describe what had happened.

I was struck by her candor, her honesty and her resolve. I was also touched by photos I was shown, pictures of her just a few months or a few years before the accident—at her daughter's wedding in 2010 in Ukraine, at Dariya's house sitting with her friend's young boy, at the Art Museum. The pictures showed her standing or walking outside—things she will never do again.

In those pictures, her dark hair and stylish glasses frame a face at peace with the world and blue eyes that seem to sparkle. Now, sitting in front of me in a hospital bed, unable to get up without the assistance of one or two aides, struggling at times to breathe without the help of a ventilator, she hardly showed any resemblance to those pictures.

Her hair was gray, her face drawn and pinched, and through those same glasses her eyes appeared troubled, hurt and disappointed. Her story was a personal nightmare that she relived constantly as she sat in a bed in a hospital or rehab center with little else to do.

"The beam was a little bit above me so I could move like that," she said, gesturing and moving her arms slightly. "And my limbs, my legs were pinned down. And I couldn't move away from that place. [There] was a little crack there, a blue little crack, and through that crack the light and the air was coming in. And somewhere it was a little bit wet and I wetted myself with that water because it was very hard. I didn't have anything to breathe with."

She recalled how she heard what was going on above, engines from the fire trucks and equipment on scene, voices from rescue workers who were frantically sifting through the rubble. But no one heard her calls for help. Haltingly and through an interpreter, she continued to tell her haunting story.

"I heard the voices. . . . They started to move things around, then I had a hope that, I had a hope that they will save me. And I was there for a long time, I was screaming, 'Help, help.' But nobody heard me. And I remember everything. I heard how everybody worked, how when they stopped working and sit down, where they left and weren't there at that moment. And the engines would stop working, I would hear everything."

Think about thirteen hours out of your day. You leave for your job at 7 a.m. Maybe it's an hour's commute to your office or your school or wherever it is that you work. You have a cup of coffee. Maybe a Danish. You take some calls. Handle whatever assignments you have. You go to lunch. Back to work in the afternoon. More calls. More interaction with co-workers, customers, students, whatever your avocation. Your work day ends at 4 p.m. Maybe you stop somewhere to meet a friend, or do some quick shopping at a market. You're home by 5 p.m. You or someone you love makes dinner. You sit down to eat. Maybe watch the news on television or check the internet after dinner. By 8 p.m. you may be sitting on the couch, finally relaxed and unwound from a busy day.

Take that slice of time, 7 a.m. to 8 p.m., in your daily life. Think about all the things you do and say and hear. That's thirteen hours. That's how long Mariya Plekan, stuck in what her rescuer would describe as a baseball catcher's crouch—a deep squatting position—was under the rubble, buried alive and wondering if anyone would ever find her. Most physically fit people can barely be in that position for a few minutes when doing exercises—let alone thirteen hours!

She knew they were out there, and she had the presence of mind, even with the pain and the fear and the agony, to realize that her only chance was to get someone's attention. So she saved her strength. When the engines and the heavy equipment were in play, when she knew her voice could not be heard, she remained silent, listening and hoping.

"I heard the barking of the dogs and I was screaming constantly when . . . the engines weren't running," she would explain. "I was screaming, 'Help, help.' But there was no help coming. And I was praying, praying, 'God, help me,' so I could be found."

And then it happened.

"I heard, I don't know when, I couldn't figure out what time, I couldn't figure out how long I've been there because it was so hard for me. I heard the dog was barking and coming up. And I started to scream 'help' again, and the dog followed my yell. And the man, I don't know who he is, he said, he came up closer with the dog. And the dog was barking at that spot and I was screaming 'help.' And he said, and he said, I heard, 'There is somebody alive here.' And they started pulling things apart and they pulled me out. And I didn't realize that it was night because the spotlights were on. I was so happy that I was saved. And I didn't know that my legs were dead at that time."

She thought she had been screaming, but as Captain O'Neill would recall, the voice was soft and almost mechanical. Thirteen hours had taken its toll on her body, her mind and her vocal cords.

"I was scared . . . so scared," she said, recalling the relief coupled with pain and fear as the rescuer workers began the delicate job of extricating her from the rubble. "As they pulled me out, I wanted to get up, but I was told, 'Don't, you cannot.'"

She said she asked why and O'Neill told her, "Because your legs are swollen."

What followed was a blur, a seventy-two-hour marathon of pain and agony and operations and medical procedures and suffering.

"Constant pain," Mariya Plekan later said in a voice resigned to a situation that was both horrifying and mortifying.

"I was so embarrassed because I was constantly open to everybody," she said. "And I had a normal comprehension because it was—and that I was so discomforted. Pain, pain, pain. And that pain is still going on."

It was pain, she said, "of the flesh."

But it was also pain of "my soul."

The medical charts told some of that story; the amputations, kidney failure that required dialysis, the inability to breathe that led to a ventilator and to tubes being inserted into her windpipe. For several months she would be unable to speak. She would gag on secretions that built up as she slept, which put her at high risk of choking to death on her own sputum.

As the case evolved, I became Mariya's advocate not only in the courtroom, but also at the hospital and nursing home. My litigation specialty is mostly medical malpractice. My familiarity with the medical system made it easier for me to monitor her care—which was excellent—and track the ups and downs of her condition. My background and experience enabled me to speak the same language as the medical and caregiving staffs. That worked to Mariya's advantage and helped ensure her proper care. The hospital providers were also familiar with me, with my line of work and perhaps with other hospital-related cases I had been involved in, so there was mutual cooperation and respect.

The media had dubbed her the "Miracle on Market Street." But there was a dark side to that miraculous rescue, and that was what would drive my legal work on her behalf.

For a time, as I mentioned earlier, doctors were not sure she would make it. But through their hard and untiring work, she reached a point where survival was no longer the issue. Living, however, was.

"Every day I have concerns and worries," she told me when I asked. "I think about everything because I have a normal memory and I have a normal understanding how I am living right now. And every day I understand how hard it is to be without legs. When you cannot take care of yourself, when you constantly depend on other people to take care of you, and I do not know how to live after that because it's so hard for me. And I'm so scared. But the doctors say there is no concerns for my life [expectancy] anymore. But I'm still scared. How am I going to be, how I need the help every day, every second."

Her children and her granddaughter kept her going.

"Because of them I want to live," she said. "I want to live. But it's so hard."

During my first visit, my discussion with one of the attending doctors was frequently interrupted by the rush of other providers reacting to medical alarms that were heard above the whooshing reverberation of her ventilator. In my line of work, trial lawyers frequently see the suffering of victims. But this experience was beyond anything I had ever witnessed. I felt sickened thinking that, in less than a minute on that fateful shopping day, Mariya's existence had been irreparably changed. I also thought about the unimaginable physical and mental deterioration she must have suffered during the time she was helplessly trapped. It seemed that Mariya would either end up dying at a relatively young age or survive but lose every enjoyable element of her life.

This was a catastrophe that was preventable. There was no doubt of that. But the more important questions were who would ultimately be found responsible and how it would be humanly possible to ensure compensation for this so terribly injured woman.

My major objective at our first meeting was to be formally retained by Mariya, and I believed I was not the only trial lawyer under consideration. Before a client agrees to hire you in a high-profile case, you usually address at least these three basic questions:

1. What is your relevant training and experience?
2. What is your assessment of the case and plan of action?
3. Will you succeed and what will the client get?

Most important, a client *must* believe that you will *always* act in their best interest—and you *must always* do so, without equivocation or exception. I've always believed that an attorney/client relationship built on a bedrock of trust and loyalty is a formula for success. Our discussion centered on my reputation for success in a courtroom as well as my unyielding allegiance to my clients. My assurance that I would *not* represent any other victims was essential in Mariya's decision making. As to my assessment of the case, regardless of Mayor Nutter's rush to judgment, I explained that it made no sense that the Salvation Army would stay open for business in light of potentially hazardous demolition next door.

Sure, neighboring buildings in the city have been safely demolished in other instances, but the Salvation Army held the keys and could have easily avoided risk by briefly closing the store until the demolition was done. After all, if the store were closed, no one would have been hurt or killed. In my mind, it was that simple.

I didn't see how anyone could effectively argue to the contrary. In fact, Richard Basciano would say as much when he complained about the Salvation Army's failure to take up his offer to swap properties. Basciano, of course, had his own agenda. He wanted to shift blame.

I knew there was more than enough blame to go around. But I needed to make sure that the Salvation Army was first in line. From a legal and public-perception standpoint, the pursuit of the Salvation Army, a well-respected charity, might be viewed as an insurmountable challenge because we would be suing the "good guys."

But in a court of law, where everyone is supposed to be judged on the evidence and not on public perception, I was willing to take my chances. For years I had successfully litigated cases against other very well-respected individuals and entities in our society. More specifically, for decades I have represented victims of medical negligence often attributed to renowned doctors at some of the most preeminent hospitals in the United States.

Contrary to popular belief, doctors and hospitals win the overwhelming majority of medical malpractice cases in Pennsylvania and many other states. And for good reason—doctors generally help cure people who are already sick and assist in their recovery from all sorts of illnesses. Most doctors are also generally well respected in our world because they are intelligent, well educated and hardworking. Thus, to successfully criticize a doctor requires a certain skill set and level of expertise that is distinguishable from efforts to impose liability for personal injuries against a large corporation, landowner or contractor.

Given my experience in the difficult field of medical malpractice, I was confident I could convince Philadelphia jurors to hold an organization, even a revered charity, to the same safety standards that apply to any other profitable retail operator. My initial research revealed that the Salvation Army was certainly profitable, with a net worth in excess of $10 billion. Conversely, at this early stage, it was apparent that other potentially responsible parties had insufficient insurance and/or assets to satisfy a substantial monetary judgment. Simply put, the Salvation Army had deep pockets. No other defendant, with the possible exception of Basciano and his company, STB Investments, offered the hope of paying any significant kind of judgment or settlement. Campbell and Benschop, who had quickly emerged as the public and political scapegoats, were virtually destitute, and that was obvious from day one.

Going into this litigation, I knew that if I did not prevail against the Salvation Army, Mariya Plekan would be left with little or nothing. Her medical bills were already in excess of $1 million, and the long-term, indeed lifetime, care she would need would require millions more. Even better, I believed in my heart that the Salvation Army was the most at fault—because all they had to do was temporarily close the store.

Although Dariya was my initial contact with Mariya, it was abundantly clear, at our first meeting, that Mariya was listening very carefully to what I had to say, and that she was the ultimate decision maker. I could tell from the discussion, as interpreted by Dariya, that Mariya respected and trusted me. (Later Mariya would tell me that, from the very beginning, she felt as though I was more than just her lawyer—that I really cared about her.) Although I could feel good karma in the room, I wasn't sure if she would make her decision that day or defer until she had an opportunity to meet with other attorneys. Then she told me she wanted me to be her lawyer. I was thrilled and honored, but I was also struck with an overwhelming sense of responsibility. Would I be able to deliver? Would I be successful in pursuing a party that had the financial resources but might ultimately prove to have no liability?

Mariya signed our firm's contingent fee agreement that day. While some lawyers in similar circumstances might request a forty or even fifty percent gross fee agreement, I offered Mariya a modest net-one-third contingent fee agreement that would never change despite the protracted and extremely challenging litigation that would follow. As I left the hospital that day, I started to reflect further and was pinching myself. After all, I was now representing the most seriously injured victim in what was likely to be one of the most memorable cases in Philadelphia history!

I knew it would be a battle, but I had no idea of the overwhelming obstacles we would face for the next four and a half years. Despite conflicting sound bites from Mayor Nutter, the DA's office, the media and even lawyers who represented some of the victims, I believed the Salvation Army was in the best position to protect the customers and employees of that store. Under Pennsylvania law, the owner/operator of a retail business bears a high degree of obligation to protect its customers. Regardless of its charitable works, the Salvation Army had that legal responsibility.

My pursuit of the Salvation Army would be met with stark opposition on multiple levels, including public opinion, but I learned as a young lawyer to focus on objectives relating to your client's needs, regardless of the fallout.

Indeed, my mentor, the late James E. Beasley, one of the best and most successful civil litigators in the country, would frequently remind me that "litigation is not a popularity contest, Andy—never forget that."

It's not difficult to follow this professional mantra against opposing counsel, but I never imagined that certain lawyers for the victims, who included close personal friends, would at times be challenging adversaries. In any event, Mariya Plekan, the most catastrophically injured survivor, needed my unrelenting advocacy, and I was determined I would not let her down.

CHAPTER FIVE

THREE WEEKS AFTER the wall went down, Danny Johnson died.

Johnson, a fifty-nine-year-old truck driver, had been shopping in the Thrift Store. He was buried under the rubble for about an hour before being pulled out and rushed to the hospital. Johnson's legs were crushed, and medical reports indicated he had suffered a heart attack. For a man with an existing heart condition who also was asthmatic, the time spent buried in the dusty rubble was life-threatening. Johnson was at Hahnemann University Hospital for nine days before he was sent home. On June 26, he was rushed back to the hospital. He died two days later.

He was to be the seventh fatality as the city continued to grapple with what had happened and why.

From a political standpoint, it appeared no one in government was willing to accept any responsibility. The primary goal, it seemed, was to find someone outside of City Hall to blame. Mayor Nutter continued to insist that the event was an aberration. The District Attorney's Office had a criminal grand jury up and running, with Griffin Campbell and the already-arrested Sean Benschop as the primary targets. OSHA's role involved conducting an independent probe, but like the mayor and the District Attorney, its focus seemed to be on the two contractors.

The Philadelphia City Council analyzed what had happened and what the City's role and possible responsibility might have been. Those issues were discussed during five separate hearings, which ran through July and August. In a city dominated by one political party—Republicans are a distinct minority and have representation on City Council only because of electoral rules that guarantee minority representation—it would be highly unlikely for an elected body to find fault with the status quo. In 1903, crusading journalist Lincoln Steffens famously described Philadelphia as "simply the most corrupt and the most contented" city in America. While that description would be extreme today, it remains true that few in government want to make waves or raise questions about their political colleagues.

The death and destruction of June 5, 2013, forced the issue. And to its credit, City Council responded. The result of its hearings was a sixty-nine-page report that included seventy-one recommended changes in the way demolition permits were issued and demolition projects were monitored. Some of the recommendations were shocking only because it was hard to believe such commonsense regulations weren't already in place. Among other things, the Council report said that any company applying for a demolition permit should include a demolition plan and proof that it was qualified to do demolition work. An applicant would also have to demonstrate that its taxes were up to date and that it did not owe the City for any prior construction work contracts, permits or other licenses.

The hearings, which received widespread media coverage, included testimony from two former commissioners of the Department of Licenses and Inspections. Ironically, Mayor Nutter was reluctant to allow current City officials from L&I or the Fire Department to appear before Council. It should be noted that Robert Mongeluzzi was one of the people who provided helpful testimony about how to improve the system.

The Department of Licenses and Inspections has had, at best, a checkered past despite efforts by respected individuals to rectify this situation. Too often the department has been run and staffed by political appointees whose allegiance is to the Mayor's Office and the Democratic Party rather than to the residents of the city. Bribes, payoffs and other shenanigans have helped underscore Lincoln Steffens' assessment.

In the 1990s one high-ranking L&I official was indicted—and eventually jailed—in a corruption probe that included charges that, while supposedly "inspecting" go-go bars and gentleman's clubs, he was actually accepting free meals, drinks and lap dances in exchange for looking the other way when it came to code violations.

A wink and a nod.

Business as usual.

Factors touched on during the Council hearings were a lack of resources for L&I, understaffing and an attitude that L&I could be an income generator for the city rather than an agency whose primary goal was to ensure safety and compliance. Testimony and evidence that surfaced during the hearings said a lot about the way the department was run and about what the priorities of the current administration really were. One fundamental question was why L&I, a supposed watchdog organization set up to monitor compliance with building and construction rules and regulations, was placed under the direction of the Deputy Mayor for Economic Development.

That Deputy Mayor, Alan Greenberger, and his top assistant, John Mondlak, were the City officials who appeared to be copied on the emails sent by STB during its dispute with the Salvation Army over the demolition project and access to the Thrift Store roof.

The City Council hearings, while inconclusive, provided some great theater and media sound bites.

For instance, Council got an interesting perspective from Bennett Levin, who had served as L&I Commissioner during the first term of Mayor Ed Rendell back in the 1990s. Never shy and always opinionated, Levin set the tone for his appearance when he told members of the media, "I'm here to speak for dead people."

"We got six dead people, a lady with no legs and an inspector who put a gun to his head," Levin said in testimony that went to the dramatic heart of what had happened.

He then described in no uncertain terms what he called a flawed system that historically had put people at risk. The Department of Licenses and Inspections, he said, "can no longer be a political backwater where money talks and people die. . . . Until you free the department from political chicanery, there's gonna be a problem. . . . Someone in the city has to finally stand up and say, 'Enough!'"

Levin pointed to several earlier tragedies in which the City and L&I did a less than credible job. In 1991 there was a fire at One Meridian Plaza, a high-rise office building across the street from City Hall. Three firemen died fighting that blaze, which raged out of control for nearly nineteen hours, in part because the sprinkler systems failed and the standpipes that were to supply water for firefighters were the wrong size. As a result, there was not enough water to fight the blaze.

In May 2000, three young women died and dozens of others were injured in the infamous Pier 34 collapse. The then ninety-one-year-old pier, located on the Delaware River near historic Penn's Landing, had been built as a loading dock area for steamships back in the day.

It no longer was a viable marine enterprise, but the farthest end of the pier had been converted into a nightclub, Club Heat. At 8 p.m. on May 18, 2000, a week after the club opened, the pier collapsed into the river.

The three women who died, all in their twenties, were co-workers who had gone to the club to celebrate a birthday. They drowned, trapped under water as the pier fell in around them. Dozens of others managed to survive and either swam to shore or were pulled out of the river.

How and why the City had issued permits allowing the club to open and what role L&I had played in that process were part of the criminal and civil litigation that followed. Allegations that the owners had failed to properly maintain and repair the ancient pier's foundation, despite warnings that the structure was unsound, were at the heart of the controversy.

Levin's testimony also touched on another tragedy linked to questionable inspection work. On October 9, 1997, Common Pleas Court Judge Berel Caesar was walking along Broad Street not far from City Hall when bolts from an eighteen-foot-high parking sign came loose from a garage wall. The falling sign struck Judge Caesar. He died four days later.

Those who were following the Salvation Army story and who knew some of the background of the Judge Caesar tragedy were struck by the irony. The garage was owned by the estate of the late Samuel A. Rappaport, who had died in 1994. Rappaport was a real estate "developer" who was also described in the media as one of the city's biggest "slumlords." At the time of his death, he was said to own more than fifty buildings, many in the Center City area, several with historic significance and more than a few in stages of disrepair.

His holdings were valued at more than $56 million and at one point included some properties on or near a disreputable Arch Street corridor that included peep shows and adult bookstores. Some of those businesses were linked to a South Jersey figure with suspected mob ties.

When Rappaport died, a good friend of his was appointed executor of his estate and was overseeing the properties at the time the garage parking sign fell and killed Judge Caesar.

That good friend was Richard Basciano.

Basciano, who once described Rappaport as a mentor, was a close friend of the family. Rappaport's children, according to one media report, referred to him as "Uncle Ritchie." Basciano's relationship with the Rappaport family eventually soured. He was removed as executor in 2002 and named in a suit filed by the family that raised questions about nearly $10 million in disbursements from the estate.

The family of Judge Caesar was awarded a $5.25 million settlement after filing a wrongful death lawsuit. The lawyer who handled that litigation and who deposed Basciano for that case is a friend of mine, Steve Wigrizer. He would be on the other side of the courtroom from Basciano (and the Salvation Army) in our litigation as well, representing the families of Mary Simpson and Roseline Conteh, two of the victims killed in the Thrift Store tragedy. Steve is a very talented, level-headed and "down to earth" lawyer who has a way of getting along with everyone.

While City Council took five days of hearings over two months to focus on the issues, Inga Saffron, the Pulitzer Prize–winning architecture critic for the *Philadelphia Inquirer*, captured the political and governmental essence of the case in an article written on June 6, 2013, the day after the tragedy. Under the headline *Changing Skyline: Building owners share similar cases of deadly neglect*, Saffron wrote about the Rappaport-Basciano connection and the City's longstanding and abject failure to deal with the problems they and others like them had created.

"Richard Basciano and the late Samuel A. Rappaport were friends, business partners, and slumlords," Saffron wrote. "Both rose from humble beginnings to become real estate speculators extraordinaire. They scooped up blighted properties in Philadelphia and sat on them for years while the structures crumbled, eventually selling them at huge markups to be developed by others."

Saffron went on, "Now they have something else in common. Both owned buildings that killed. While the circumstances of the two fatal accidents are very different, the cases are linked by more than just the two men's complex relationship; the tragedies reveal the City's inability to enforce basic building safety. And it's not just the Nutter administration. For more than 30 years, every mayor . . . has exhibited a stunningly high level of tolerance for the blight the two men wrought."

Responding to critics, Mayor Nutter, who would order a separate investigation into the tragedy, added that the Department of Licenses and Inspections in 2013 had a more qualified staff, improved technology and streamlined processes for dealing with issues than at any time in the past.

However true the mayor's claim may have been, assigning blame and avoiding responsibility seemed to be the goal of City Hall and the District Attorney's Office as the various investigations continued. Based on its hearings, City Council issued a report on September 26, 2013, that cited shortcomings in the way the City and L&I handled construction and demolition permits. The report recommended a series of changes, but fell short of specifically attaching responsibility to anyone or any department in City Hall.

When a member of the Council committee that issued the report was asked why no individual or agency was held accountable, he replied, "That's not our department."

This sidestepping was all about public perception. Legally, it was virtually impossible to hold the City or the Department of Licenses and Inspections liable for anything that happened on June 5. The City had sovereign immunity from civil suit for its failure to inspect the ongoing demolition on Market Street. Under Pennsylvania law, the City of Philadelphia could be sued for damages only if its actions fell within one of the narrowly construed eight exceptions for which the Pennsylvania legislature had waived sovereign immunity. Those exceptions included: (1) the operation of a car by a City employee or official; (2) the care, custody and control of personal property in the City's possession; (3) the care, custody and control of real property in the City's possession; (4) the care, custody and control of trees, traffic lights, traffic signs, or street lights or signs; (5) a utility service; (6) a dangerous condition on City-owned streets; (7) a dangerous condition on City-owned sidewalks; and (8) the care, custody and control of animals. None of these exceptions applied because the City did not have full possession and control over the properties on Market Street. The City was not immune to a civil rights suit in federal court, but that was ultimately not pursued for a number of reasons, including anticipated legal challenges and a less favorable venue.

While I believed that the City could have done more and that it had played a role in the tragedy, from our perspective this did not mitigate the Salvation Army's responsibility. The Salvation Army chose to open its store for business that morning without any concern for potential danger, and therefore became liable and responsible for what happened.

Another twist in the law would surface as the civil litigation progressed. While few people outside the legal community realized it at the time, the Salvation Army employees were *barred* from having any claims for negligence and other third-party claims against their employer in light of the Pennsylvania Workers' Compensation Act. They could, however, pursue workers' compensation claims.

On November 14, two months after the Council report was released, OSHA weighed in. The federal agency cited both Campbell and Benschop for "willful, egregious violations" in the demolition project, most notably the failure to conduct a top-down demolition, which would have likely avoided a wall collapse. Campbell's construction company was fined $313,000 by OSHA. Benschop's company was fined $84,000. (Much to our chagrin, the Salvation Army was not cited.)

Given the financial status of the two men, it's unlikely either of those fines will ever be paid.

Later that same month, on November 25, a Philadelphia grand jury handed down an indictment against Griffin Campbell. The contractor, like Benschop, was charged with multiple crimes: six counts of third-degree murder, six counts of manslaughter and thirteen counts of recklessly endangering another person, causing a catastrophe and criminal conspiracy.

Seth Williams, the District Attorney, said Campbell was "at the center of culpability for the collapse," which he described as "tragic and preventable" and which he said "robbed our city of six amazing Philadelphians that perished in the rubble."

The motive for these crimes, Williams added, "was greed."

That last comment proved to be dramatically ironic. Williams left office in disgrace several years later, pleading guilty to fraud-related charges lodged against him by federal prosecutors. Among other things, Williams was accused of stealing more than $20,000 that had been set aside for nursing home expenses for his elderly and ailing mother. The District Attorney, whose time in office would be cut short by his own greed-based problems, loved the spotlight and the role of crime buster. But he proved again and again while serving as the city's top law enforcement officer that he was more interested in headlines than in justice.

None of this—the City Council report, the OSHA fines, the grand jury indictments—did anything for the families of the seven people who had died. Moreover, none would restore Mariya Plekan's ability to walk on her own two legs or to live an independent, self-sufficient life without enormous debt from overwhelming medical bills.

Justice had to be found somewhere else.

Civil litigation aimed at holding the Salvation Army, STB Investments and Basciano and his associates accountable was where the real fight for justice would be fought. Lawsuits filed by attorneys for the victims and their families began piling up in the Court of Common Pleas of Philadelphia. The defendants also included Benschop, Campbell and Campbell Construction. Judge Mark I. Bernstein was initially assigned the cases. Judge Bernstein is a highly intelligent and deeply respected jurist who has instituted a number of helpful reforms to improve the quality of efficient justice and trial by jury in Philadelphia. He has also authored an authoritative treatise on evidence. In August 2013, the lawyers for Campbell and Benschop filed motions to stay against eleven of the victims who had filed suit. The stay—a delay in the proceedings—was requested because of the active grand jury investigation. The argument, which applied to Campbell, Benschop and anyone else who might be criminally charged, was that until the criminal process had been completed, potential defendants would "have to exercise their Fifth Amendment rights" against self-incrimination and would be unable to properly respond to the civil litigation.

Judge Bernstein appropriately granted the stay.

But we had a problem. At the time I filed suit on behalf of Mariya, including the Salvation Army as a defendant, her medical condition was tenuous at best. Despite all the work done to save her life, she remained critically ill, suffering with overwhelming sepsis and renal failure. I was worried she might not survive. As a result, I filed a motion with the court seeking permission to depose my client to preserve her video testimony for trial despite the stay in the civil proceedings. Judge Bernstein granted my motion, and I was allowed to take her video deposition.

Depositions are part of an important process, known as discovery, leading up to a civil trial. Eventually all the major players and most of the minor players in the Salvation Army tragedy would be deposed—questioned under oath by attorneys representing the plaintiffs and defendants. All depositions are recorded by a court stenographer. Today many are also videotaped. They provide lawyers with an opportunity to see and hear the principal figures in the litigation. They also offer an opportunity to better prepare in advance for trial, which includes the cross-examination of witnesses. Depositions are perhaps the best discovery tool for lawyers relating to trial preparation.

While depositions are taken under oath, they are not in front of a judge. Lawyers, however, can object to questions, and those objections are placed on the record. The process can at times be adversarial, and the give-and-take is sometimes heated.

The reality is that by the time a case is ready to be put in front of a jury, there aren't many secrets if discovery has been properly conducted. Both sides usually know the key evidence and, for the most part, the testimony that will be introduced at trial. In fact, depositions serve to keep witnesses from changing their stories. A witness who says one thing under oath during a deposition and subsequently contradicts that testimony at trial in front of a jury has a significant credibility problem.

Taking depositions is like finding pieces to a puzzle. The skill of any trial lawyer is taking those puzzle pieces and creating the credible picture that will suitably present the client's story that he or she wants the jury to see.

The picture that I wanted was of Mariya Plekan before and after June 5, 2013. I wanted the jury not only to understand what had happened to her, but to see what had happened. I also wanted the jury to have a clear understanding of why it had happened and what she had lost.

And very early on—before some other plaintiff attorneys would recognize this—I wanted a picture that clearly demonstrated that the Salvation Army was primarily responsible for what had happened to her and the other victims that day. Mariya's live testimony would help establish claims relating to intentional misrepresentation and the victims' justifiable belief that the store was safe if it was open for business.

Mariya's personal account was the first step, the key puzzle piece, in creating that picture. I took her live video deposition on November 20, 2013, at Good Shepherd Rehabilitation Center in Philadelphia, where she was being cared for following her release from the hospital. Mariya was in her wheelchair hooked up to a ventilator. She told her story as compellingly as she had told it to me in private. She discussed her belief that the Salvation Army store was safe that day; otherwise, she would have expected the organization to close the store. She recounted in detail the thirteen hours she had spent under the rubble after the collapse, her desperate and agonizing attempts to call for help, the frustration she felt as rescue workers passed over her without hearing her, the drips of water that sustained her and the miraculous discovery that freed her.

And she repeated her concerns for the future, emphasizing that while her body had been broken, her mind was fully functioning.

"And every day I understand how hard it is to be without legs," she said, repeating a line that underscored her situation. When we got in front of a jury, I wanted those men and women to see and hear all of that. One of the last questions I asked of Mariya was what gave her the mental strength to stay alive.

I'll never forget her answer. Her struggle, she said, was not for herself, but for her son, her daughter and her granddaughter.

At the end of the deposition, I asked the attorneys if they had any questions. The room was completely silent. In the dozens of depositions taken in the Market Street Building Collapse Litigation over the span of several years, it turned out to be the *only* deposition where lawyers asserted *no* objections and asked *no* follow-up questions.

CHAPTER SIX

Plato Marinakos Jr. threw Griffin Campbell under the bus.

The architect who had cut a deal with the District Attorney's Office to avoid being charged in the case became the principal witness in the ongoing criminal investigation. The round-faced fifty-year-old testified before the grand jury that handed down the indictment against Campbell in November 2013. Thereafter, he made his first public appearance as a cooperating witness at a preliminary hearing, in February of the following year, where prosecutors laid out their case.

The hearing went on for four hours and ended with a judge ruling that both Campbell and Benschop should be held over for trial. It came as no surprise that neither had the financial ability to post bail, so they both remained behind bars.

Evidence and testimony at the hearing included photos and videotapes from the day of the accident, including the SEPTA bus video that captured the exact moment the adjoining wall came down and flattened the back half of the Thrift Store like a pancake.

How and why that happened and who was responsible were the issues presented to the judge during the hearing. Marinakos, whose role was crucial to any examination of the tragedy, pointed the finger at Campbell. The District Attorney apparently saw no need to look elsewhere.

"You can't leave a wall unbraced like that," Marinakos said he told Campbell on June 4. Marinakos said the collapse of the wall the following morning was a "total disaster," but he never accepted responsibility for what had happened.

His story helped establish a narrative that was embraced by City officials. Culpability and responsibility began and ended with Griffin Campbell and Sean Benschop. Again and again Marinakos would argue that he had no control over the "means and methods" of the demolition.

Campbell was the contractor hired to do the demolition, Marinakos explained, and as such he controlled the means and methods for accomplishing the job. Marinakos said his role was to oversee the project but not to dictate how the work was carried out.

Evidence introduced at the preliminary hearing centered on the five days leading up to the collapse, with particular emphasis on Marinakos's detailed account of how he had reacted on June 4 to the unbraced wall that loomed over the Thrift Store and how he had allegedly told Campbell that the wall had to come down "immediately."

He said Campbell promised to complete the task by setting up scaffolding and having a crew work through the night dismantling the wall by hand. Marinakos apparently accepted that explanation, even though the reality of the situation made that impossible. It would have been obvious to anyone who had been at the demolition site, as Marinakos had been repeatedly, that erecting scaffolding on the uneven, debris-strewn, hollowed interior of the Hoagie City building was absurd.

Still, Marinakos stuck to his story. After all, his immunity deal offered him protection from criminal prosecution. It was his buffer, his protection against anyone who might challenge or question his motives. Campbell would later allege that he had kicked back $5,000 to Marinakos after he was awarded the $112,000 demolition contract. He also alleged that the architect had provided him with information about the other bids on the job so that he would emerge as the low bidder.

Marinakos steadfastly denied those charges. The District Attorney's Office, with Williams at the helm, saw no need to pursue them. Clearly, Campbell and Benschop were the targets. Everything and everyone else were immaterial. Marinakos's role and responsibility would figure prominently, however, in the civil litigation.

The City's view of what had happened and why was outlined at the preliminary hearing by Assistant District Attorney Jennifer Selber. Selber, consistent with her assigned role as a prosecutor, focused on June 4, the night Marinakos told Campbell that the wall had to come down immediately. Selber is a highly skilled trial lawyer who handled her assignment very well.

"You have an occupied structure in the Salvation Army," she said. "Everybody knew it was going to open for business the next day. And that every customer that came in and every person that worked there was going to be in immediate danger. And then, on top of that, to operate a 36,000-pound piece of equipment [the excavator used by Benschop] that rumbles and vibrates and makes noise and bangs into the adjoining building is the epitome of recklessness."

The recklessness of the Salvation Army in deciding to keep the Thrift Store open was not part of the equation.

Selber's boss, District Attorney Seth Williams, told reporters that the grand jury investigation was continuing. But when asked about the civil litigation that pointed to Basciano and the Salvation Army, the DA said that the standard for prosecution in a criminal proceeding was higher than the threshold for suing in civil litigation.

The preliminary hearing ended with Campbell and Benschop back in jail to await trial. They were to be formally arraigned on third-degree murder, manslaughter, conspiracy and related charges in March. A trial date was expected sometime in 2015. Our civil litigation was moving slowly forward, but the reality was that we would never get in front of a civil jury until the criminal trial had been completed.

There was, however, activity in another arena—the court of public opinion.

Back in September, Nancy Winkler, the Philadelphia City Treasurer whose daughter Anne Bryan had died in the Thrift Store rubble, started an online petition to create a memorial park on the site of the collapse. Within a week she had 1,700 signatures supporting the proposal.

"The memorial park would be a fitting way to acknowledge the disaster, to assure that it will never be forgotten and to remind the citizens of Philadelphia of the need for government oversight in building demolition in order to protect public safety and human lives," Winkler said.

Mayor Nutter quickly jumped on board.

And so did the Salvation Army.

In March, around the same time Campbell and Benschop were formally arraigned, Nutter held a press conference to announce that the Salvation Army, responding to Ms. Winkler's request, had agreed to donate the Thrift Store site for the memorial park. Nutter praised the decision while Major Robert W. Dixon, a top regional Salvation Army official, stood at his side.

Because of the civil litigation, Dixon did not speak publicly. But the donation and his presence at the news conference spoke for him. The Salvation Army was staking out its position as a victim of circumstance, and its generous act of donating the property was part of the healing process. At one point the City suggested it might help the Army find another Center City location for a store.

Those of us familiar with the real story—a story lost on City officials and largely ignored by the media—could not help but shake our heads at the irony.

Another Center City location had been offered to the Salvation Army long before anyone was killed or maimed. But officials of the charitable organization, for reasons that were never made clear, had rejected the deal, i.e., the swap of properties Richard Basciano proposed.

That business decision was one of many along a path that led to suffering, death and destruction. And it underscored the point I wanted to make at the outset in the civil litigation. The Salvation Army is a charitable organization that has done and continues to do amazing work for those in need throughout the world. But that was not the controlling issue here. It was our position that the Salvation Army, in this instance, made a series of business decisions, based on economics and its own financial well-being, that put its workers and its customers at significant risk. Its adamant and seemingly inexplicable refusal to grant access to the roof of the store was a big part of the problem. Even more egregious and perplexing was its decision to keep the Thrift Store open that Wednesday morning despite the warnings that a dangerous situation existed. Our position was that the Salvation Army was simply a business entity that should be held to the same standards as other retailers. If this had been Macy's, Sears, The Gap or any other clothing store, the accountability question would have been obvious. Simply put, the Salvation Army was clearly the most at fault.

Even though they had joined our motion to compel the depositions of these defendants, not all the plaintiffs and their attorneys saw the issue as plainly as I did. As the case moved forward, we—myself and my co-counsel, Elizabeth Crawford—often found ourselves fighting battles on two fronts. We regularly clashed with the defendants' attorneys and sometimes found ourselves on the opposite side of issues from the lawyers for some of the other plaintiffs as well.

In those battles, Liz Crawford's assistance was invaluable. She worked legal issues and strategies with me throughout the case and, as important, was an ally in the disagreements in which we were often standing alone. Hers was an amazing legal performance considering she had no prior courtroom experience. She had come to work with me at Kline & Specter, P.C. in July 2013, shortly after I got involved in the case. Liz was a graduate of what is now the Thomas R. Kline School of Law at Drexel University. Tom Kline is my partner at the firm and is regarded as a top trial lawyer in Pennsylvania and the United States. The other lead partner in our firm, Shanin Specter, son of the late Senator Arlen Specter, is also a phenomenal trial lawyer. I am very fortunate to be a senior partner with Tom and Shanin, and they have been very good about giving me leeway to hire (and fire) as necessary to properly run my practice at the firm.

Although Liz was a young lawyer with only a few years' experience at the time, she had clerked for the Pennsylvania Supreme Court before joining our law firm. Moreover, she came highly recommended by my lovely wife, Gwen. Gwen, as the Director of Trial Advocacy at the law school, was Liz's professor and had started training her as a young law student. Although my wife has an excellent sense of judgment about people, I was understandably reticent when Gwen recommended Liz for the first time in April 2013. I was looking for another lawyer to work with me but assumed it would need to be a lateral hire—someone with at least five years of prior litigation experience. After all, my practice was busy. I had over seventy cases, and six were Philadelphia cases scheduled for trial in 2014. At that time, most of the lawyers at Kline & Specter were also lateral hires. Despite my initial concerns, I decided to interview Liz. While it was evident she was very bright and the Supreme Court had commended her research and writing ability, I was most impressed with her desire to learn and work hard. After checking her references, I decided to hire her. (Of interest, I found out much later she had also sent her resume to Mongeluzzi's firm the same week she interviewed with me, but she did not hear back from them.)

Aside from the challenges Liz faced as a young trial lawyer, she was also very busy at home because she had recently had a baby with her husband, Rob. Liz was always able to balance everything successfully as a trial lawyer and a mother. It should be noted that Gwen, who has always been the glue that holds our family together, had done the same with our three children while working in the prestigious law firm of White and Williams—and with flying colors! Liz had her baby in the spring of her third year of law school, went on to pass the bar exam just months later and then began a full-time job right after the bar exam. I found out quickly that she demonstrated a high level of maturity and responsibility as compared to some of her young lawyer counterparts.

It's difficult to imagine a more intense baptism by fire for a new lawyer. When she started working with me in the summer of 2013, her first assignment was to draft the civil complaint for our lawsuit. Her work was outstanding, and I continued to depend on her moving forward. I was impressed with both her work product and her work ethic. More important, I trusted her instincts. There are some things you can't learn in a classroom—especially relating to litigation and trial advocacy. Sometimes you have to go with your gut. In our situation, battling at times on several fronts, this was paramount.

What's more, Liz's presence, often in a room full of type-A, aggressive and seasoned male attorneys, provided a welcomed counterbalance. Hers was a voice of cool-headed logic and reason, in contrast to mine, which at times resorted to forceful advocacy in response to certain lawyers who sometimes acted like a pack of hyenas. Obviously, the defendants, and in particular the Salvation Army, adamantly opposed our view that their beloved charity was the most responsible. And certain plaintiffs, at the outset, showed great reluctance to focus blame on the Salvation Army for the debacle. After all, attempting to place sole blame, or the bulk of the blame, on a well-respected religious charity organization was a risky, even potentially unwinnable and destabilizing strategy. There was also a strong belief that the Salvation Army had the unequivocal support of many Philadelphia citizens.

Our hope was to convince a jury otherwise, and to emphasize the culpability of the Salvation Army. It was a major risk, but one that I felt we had to take. We represented only one client. Six people in her position that Wednesday morning had died. Mariya had also been buried alive but miraculously survived. When she walked into the store that day, she had no idea her life was about to change forever. Had the Salvation Army heeded the warnings and closed the store, those who had died would still be alive and Mariya would be standing on her own two feet.

A donation of land for a park that would memorialize the deceased victims of the tragedy was in keeping with the Army's charitable mission. But we also saw it as part of a public relations move to burnish the organization's image and take the focus away from its role—its crucial role—in the catastrophic events of June 5, 2013. As the civil litigation moved forward, I filed a motion *in limine* to preclude any defendant attorney from introducing evidence at trial that would mention the land donation and memorial park. (It should also be noted that the memorial would recognize only those who had perished—Mariya and other surviving victims would never be mentioned.)

Early in June 2014, Campbell and Benschop lost another important legal battle when the judge at a pretrial hearing refused to dismiss a conspiracy charge that went to an important aspect of the case against them. The defense attorneys argued that the two men did not set out to create a catastrophe and should not be charged with knowingly causing the tragedy. Prosecutors argued that the two men were aware of the dangers they had created but agreed to go forward without any regard for what might happen. The judge agreed and allowed the conspiracy charges to remain in the case.

Benschop's lawyer, Daine Grey, had argued that his client didn't have any control over what was going on at the demolition site, but was merely following orders from Campbell, who was running the operation.

"He did not control the means of demolition, did not control the method of demolition, he simply followed what his employer did," Grey told reporters after the hearing. "There were a number of other workers who followed instructions in taking down portions of the building that were not arrested."

The only difference, he argued, was that while those workers might have been using sledgehammers or hand claws to do demolition work, his client was using a piece of heavy equipment. Benschop, he said, was a "scapegoat."

That was one of the few points on which he and Campbell's lawyer, William Hobson, appeared to agree. Hobson portrayed Campbell as a victim betrayed by people like Marinakos, whom he had trusted and once considered a friend. He also cast his client as an outsider who did not move in the same political and social circles, or have the connections and economic status, as people like Basciano and the officials at the Salvation Army.

"Griff Campbell is not the kind of guy that's going to be invited to $1,000-a-plate fundraisers," said Hobson.

Three days after that hearing, on June 5, 2014, the first anniversary of the tragedy, a groundbreaking ceremony was held for the memorial park at the 22nd and Market Street site. City officials and friends and family members of the victims attended the event. At one point Mayor Nutter broke down in tears as he embraced family members of those who had died.

"I can very easily speak for all Philadelphians, people in the region, many across the country, and some around the world in saying that our hearts are still broken a year later," he said. "This was one of the worst tragedies that our city has experienced in modern times."

"Our message today is to thank everyone for recognizing that this was the right thing to do," Nancy Winkler said. "We would like a beautiful park that reflects the importance of human life." There was never any question that Ms. Winkler and her husband Jay were loving and devoted parents who were desolate at the loss of their beautiful daughter.

The ceremony received full media coverage and became part of numerous one-year-later stories in newspapers, on television and on radio. A report from 6ABC, the ABC affiliate in Philadelphia, offered some of the perspective that Nutter's comments clearly lacked, alluding to the City's failure to oversee the demolition work, noting that "the system collapsed long before that wall" and calling the lack of oversight a "systemic failure."

In September 2014, the Mayor's Special Independent Advisory Commission, set up in the wake of the June 5 collapse, issued a ninety-six-page report on the Department of Licenses and Inspections. Titled "Safety First and Foremost," the report alluded to the problems cited in the media, but in softer tones. The twenty-two-member panel found that Licenses and Inspections "was a bureaucracy struggling to support an ever-expanding workload in a climate of constantly shrinking budgets with tentacles reaching deep into almost every aspect of City life. The disparate assignments it was given often conflicted, frequently confusing the City residents who needed to use L&I services as well as those who provided them."

The report included a series of recommendations, including the establishing of a Department of Buildings to better oversee some of the problems cited. It also proposed better City management of vacant and abandoned properties, stricter regulations for demolition work, better staffing and training for L&I employees, tighter financial controls and better coordination between the City's Law Department and L&I.

The report noted that although there was "insufficient evidence to determine whether any administrative misconduct occurred," there were clear indications that "the City did not respond to several warnings that the demolition was a dangerous operation that could lead to dire consequences."

It appeared that Mayor Nutter and others got just what they asked for. Changes in regulations and procedures, enacted and signed into law in the wake of the commission report and the City Council hearings, gave politicians the platform to announce that they had addressed the problems.

That those problems had existed for years and had not been looked at until seven people were killed and twelve others injured or maimed was not on anyone's agenda.

In a clear reference to Basciano's operations along Market Street, the commission report noted that, in early 2013, "the south side of Market Street, between 21st and 22nd Streets, was occupied by a set of rundown buildings that had once been a hub of the sex industry. Since at least the 1970s, porn shops, peep shows and 'massage parlors' with flashing neon signs, came to life after dark."

But "progress was closing in as new office and apartment towers were going up and older buildings were given new life." The report went on to question the ease with which Campbell was able to obtain demolition permits despite his lack of experience, the spotty inspections conducted by both L&I and OSHA, and the disregard for the warnings contained in the emails between STB and the Salvation Army. While suggesting a failure to heed the danger signs, the report came up short in fixing responsibility or accessing global accountability.

In the wake of the report, Campbell and Benschop were once again the targets. Were they scapegoats? Had they acted criminally? Or were they simply incompetent and grossly negligent? Those questions cast a shadow over our civil litigation. I knew we had to get beyond the low hanging fruit that City officials like the DA and the mayor found so easy to pick. I believed it was fair to question the competence of Campbell and Benschop and to ask if they had been negligent. But to this day, and based in large part on how much I know about this case, I find it difficult to label their actions criminal. Others agree with my view, but I recognize there is room for disagreement.

The civil case finally got underway at full tilt in the fall of 2014. The lawyers in the case included some of the most experienced and well-known litigators in the city. The plaintiffs' side included Bob Mongeluzzi. Mongeluzzi represented the families of three of those who had died as well as six people who had been injured. He is an experienced construction litigation attorney. He was described on his own law firm's website as "the most respected and successful construction accident attorney in the United States." A profile that appeared on NBC10, the local NBC affiliate, in April 2013, just two months before the Market Street building collapse, referred to him as the "Master of Disasters" and the "King of Construction Accidents." Before our civil case began, Bob Mongeluzzi, or "Mongo" as he is commonly known, was a good friend of mine; that changed by the time the case was over. Mongeluzzi was assisted by his younger partner, Jeff Goodman, a bright young trial lawyer who feels comfortable in court and is always prepared.

Steve Wigrizer is also a highly experienced trial lawyer who has achieved significant success during his illustrious legal career, including his representation of Judge Caesar's estate, as mentioned earlier. Steve is well grounded and reasoned in his approach to problems, and it's rare that Steve loses his temper. Steve was assisted by his associate, Jason Weiss, a proficient young lawyer who honed his legal skills as the case progressed. Harry Roth is another noteworthy plaintiff lawyer best known for his legal acumen and diligence, and he has also enjoyed a number of substantial accomplishments during his many years of practice. Adam Grutzmacher is a young, earnest and hard-working lawyer. Both Roth and Grutzmacher represented victims who were employed by the Salvation Army, and, as will be discussed, were not legally permitted to pursue direct claims against the Army because of the Pennsylvania Workers' Compensation Act. Jerome Gamburg and his son Robert also had significant involvement in the case, relating to an important liability witness and plaintiff—the store manager, Margarita Agosto. Jerry has a ton of valuable trial experience (from about sixty years of law practice), and his son Robert, who also handles criminal matters, is also an accomplished and zealous advocate for his clients.

Of the lawyers on the defense side, top on the list was Basciano's attorney, Richard A. Sprague. Richard Sprague is one of the most famous and highly regarded lawyers not only in Philadelphia but across the country. He has an outstanding national reputation. He had been a prosecutor, a defense attorney and had worked on the investigations into the assassinations of John F. Kennedy and Martin Luther King, Jr. At eighty-nine, he was still active and still held in the highest esteem by attorneys throughout the city. Despite his age, he still displays a keen mind and perspicacious wit. Simply put, Sprague is one of the top "old-school" trial lawyers in the United States—a true legal hall of famer. Interestingly enough, Sprague had been a close friend of my mentor, James E. Beasley, before Beasley passed on September 18, 2004.

During the litigation, Dick Sprague worked closely with his astute son, Tom, a partner at his law firm of Sprague & Sprague. Tom is also an outstanding lawyer, intelligent, poised, ethical and prepared; he's learned a lot from his father but is a success in his own right. Tom became a primary player in the case, and he was a point person on many issues for the defense. Peter Greiner was also part of the Sprague team. Sort of a tough guy on the exterior but very smart, Greiner had a lot of passion relating to the representation of his clients, and I respected that.

Going up against Richard Sprague presents both a challenge and an opportunity. The challenge is attempting to match wits and strategy with an opponent whom you both respect and admire. The opportunity is the chance to learn good and sometimes hard lessons. Interestingly enough, shortly after the death of my friend and mentor Jim Beasley Sr., I had left the Beasley firm in 2005 to join Kline & Specter as a partner. Much to my surprise (because I really didn't think I was that important), the news media stories went viral when I left. Richard Sprague was promptly retained by the Beasley firm, and litigation followed on the heels of my departure. This was portrayed as an evolving drama in the newspapers, and it is a story in itself; in summary, the case settled amicably almost as quickly as it started. Despite the short span of that litigation, I can tell you from firsthand knowledge that being pursued by Richard Sprague in litigation is anything but a pleasant experience! Through the years, I must admit that I was not a fan of Mr. Sprague, but during the course of the Market Street trial, I got to see many things that I truly admired, including the way he and Tom bonded as well as their skillful and successful representation of Mr. Basciano and his related companies.

In addition to the Sprague firm, the Market Street Building Collapse Litigation, as it was referred to in most court documents, was chock full of other high-profile defense lawyers. First and foremost were Jack Snyder and Bill Carr of the traditional and celebrated Rawle & Henderson law firm. Snyder is a very assertive, tall and distinguished-looking trial lawyer with years of successful experience under his belt. Carr, his partner, offered invaluable assistance to Snyder and did a very effective job in his own right. Also part of the Salvation Army legal team was John Hare, a highly intelligent and insightful appellate lawyer, who was always feeding Snyder with the necessary legal ammunition to help fight his battles. Marinakos was represented by Neil Clain, Jr., a skilled and clever trial lawyer who had his hands full representing a very culpable architect. Also notable was a younger lawyer, Bryan Werley, who represented Griffin Campbell in the civil case by calmly and deftly presenting his side of the story, using a soft and yet convincing tone. Sean Benschop had no legal counsel in the civil case and so, for all intents and purposes, was unrepresented.

On October 6, 2014, the discovery phase of the litigation began in earnest with Mongeluzzi questioning Plato Marinakos. Mongeluzzi was representing more victims than any other plaintiff lawyer. Of the nine litigants he represented, three were Salvation Army employees. Because it was anticipated that the court would likely rule that all Salvation Army victims were barred under the Workers' Compensation Act from pursuing any negligence-related claims against their employer, it was in the best financial interest of the employees that Basciano, STB and Marinakos be held accountable. In other words, from a monetary standpoint, the potential liability of the Salvation Army had no impact on them. Our position, of course, was to focus on the Salvation Army. Yet I believed that my representation of Mariya would help all the litigants, including the group of Mongeluzzi's clients who were not Salvation Army workers. My client's catastrophic injuries—and the defendants' fear of the impact those injuries might have on an award of damages—constituted a serious risk for all the defendants, and that would work to everyone's advantage.

Under oath for a third time, Marinakos told the same story at his deposition that he had told the criminal grand jury and that he had repeated from the witness stand at the preliminary hearing. But this time he was a target, not a cooperator. He was aggressively questioned in detail by Bob Mongeluzzi, who appeared to be following lines of inquiry that placed the architect and Richard Basciano in his crosshairs and essentially ignored most other parties, including the Salvation Army.

It was understandable that holding Marinakos responsible might provide some satisfaction, but from where we stood, that was only part of the story. At best he was a buffer for Basciano and a turncoat when it came to Campbell and Benschop. His agreement to cooperate and his immunity deal in many ways had protected both him and his employer from criminal prosecution.

Mongeluzzi effectively led the charge against Marinakos, Basciano, STB, Campbell and Benschop while Liz Crawford and I consistently focused our attack on the Salvation Army.

From the point of view of those actively pursing the architect, if Marinakos had failed professionally in his duties overseeing the project, then the line of accountability would run up the ladder to those who had hired him and for whom he was working. But the liability of these parties in the civil litigation was something that I *consistently* wanted to downplay throughout the discovery phase and ultimately the trial. Anything that shifted the focus away from the Salvation Army was, in our estimation, not in the best interest of our client or in the best pursuit of justice.

Marinakos's deposition was like a fifteen-round boxing match. It went on for several days. During this verbal fistfight, the architect tried to bob and weave. When he was asked if the unbraced wall was "a danger," he replied, "It could be dangerous."

When he was asked about Campbell's demolition being front-to-back rather than top-to-bottom, he said, "I knew he was going front to back, but I didn't see that as an issue."

At another point he said, "I didn't get into the whole—the nitty gritty of the means and methods on how to take the wall down because [Campbell] was in control of that."

Sounding themes that would become part of the Basciano/STB defense, Marinakos said that none of the problems would have arisen "if he [Campbell] took care of the wall like I told him," nor, he added, would this have been an issue if the Salvation Army had taken Basciano's offer to exchange the Thrift Store for "a bigger building, a nicer building."

The architect also emphasized that he wasn't at the accident site that morning, so he couldn't say for certain what had caused the wall to come down. But in response to a question on that topic, he said, "Let me explain something. The wall wasn't a thin little wall of one width of brick. It was a substantial wall, at least four to five, maybe six bricks thick. So, I mean, I'm not an engineer, like I said, but I'm not—I don't think a little vibration from a subway could have made the wall collapse."

Marinakos, as he had in his previous testimony, said that Campbell had promised him on June 4 that he would take the wall down that night. The next morning, he said, in a phone call around 9 a.m., he had asked Campbell if the wall was down and was told that it was.

"He lied," Marinakos said.

That raised several eyebrows. It was pointed out that Basciano was there that morning and that Campbell knew Marinakos intended to stop by. Why would Campbell lie about the wall being down if he knew Basciano was there and Marinakos would be there shortly?

"I don't know," Marinakos said. "You have to ask Griffin Campbell."

In fact, Campbell would tell a decidedly different story in describing the events that took place that morning, but we wouldn't hear that story until he took the stand at his own criminal trial.

What the Marinakos deposition demonstrated was the line of defense that he, Basciano and STB intended to set up in the civil litigation. The Salvation Army would also, in part, join in that defense. Not everything he said, however, put the people he was working for in the best light.

There was discussion, for example, about a scissors high-reach, a heavy piece of equipment that could have been used to effectively take the wall down. Neither it, nor the aerial lift suggested by Benschop, had been employed to deal with the unbraced wall that was the cause of so much concern in Marinakos's emails.

Marinakos conceded that a scissors high-reach had been used early in the demolition work to save what was described as "ornate, carved scroll work" that was part of the façade on one of the other buildings. The façade was saved because Thomas Simmonds, the STB project manager in New York, wanted it.

The implication was clear. STB was willing to spend money for a heavy piece of equipment to save an ornate façade, but not to safely take down a wall that was dangerously looming over the Thrift Store.

Marinakos tried to paint himself as a man caught in the middle. He said his emails in the weeks leading up to the collapse were an attempt to solve the problem. But he acknowledged that he was less than successful. "You had STB on one side and you had the Salvation Army on the other side," he said. "And they wouldn't listen to each other."

"It was a game of chicken, sir, wasn't it?" Marinakos was asked of the emails that were flying back and forth between STB and the Salvation Army.

Again, the architect tried to dodge the question. "That's not the characterization . . . I was trying to get . . . to have cooler heads to prevail."

Finally, Marinakos described the phone call he received at 10:42 a.m. on June 5, 2013, from Griffin Campbell. "He was frantic," Marinakos said. "He said the building had collapsed and I should get to the site right away."

Three minutes later, Simmonds was on the phone telling him virtually the same thing. Simmonds was in New York. How did he find out so fast? Marinakos was asked.

He didn't know the answer. But it was a question that would come up again as the civil litigation moved forward and plaintiff attorneys began to challenge Richard Basciano's convoluted account of where he was and what he did when the wall came down that morning.

All of that would be dealt with later.

"I was shell-shocked," Marinakos said in describing his reaction to the initial phone call from Campbell and the subsequent call from Simmonds. "I didn't understand what had happened at the site. . . . I don't remember exactly the call I had with Tom [Simmonds]."

What he did remember, he said, was the chaos and destruction when he arrived at 22nd and Market Streets that morning.

"It was terrible," he said. "It was . . . there was firemen everywhere, people were on the sidewalk. It was a horrific scene."

Marinakos said police barricades made it difficult for him to get close, but that he worked his way around to Market Street, where he found Griffin Campbell and asked what had happened.

"He said . . . the wall collapsed. He grabbed . . . the excavator grabbed something, or, you know, pulled on something and the whole building fell down. . . . I was shocked. . . . It was terrible."

While Mongeluzzi spent days questioning and debating Marinakos at his deposition, I was brief and focused when I finally got a chance to question him. Proving his liability or that of Basciano, STB Investments, Campbell and Benschop was not my primary concern. Instead, I wanted to use Marinakos's own words to underscore what we believed was a contributing cause of the tragedy—the Salvation Army's failure to provide Campbell access to the roof. Access was the basis of all the "warning emails" that led up to the collapse of the wall, and Marinakos had involvement with the access issue. I wanted to be sure that his answers to my questions would help our case against the Army. The point we needed to put in front of a jury was that, had access been given, the collapse might not have happened. And *only* the Salvation Army was in a position to grant that access.

At one point Marinakos told me he thought an access agreement was going to be reached. And he agreed when I suggested that "there was interest in having access to that roof that went on for weeks before the actual collapse."

Safety concerns and a desire to protect the roof from any damage during demolition were the reasons that STB had cited repeatedly in asking for access, he said, agreeing with my assessment that "they wanted to make sure they could take that adjoining party wall down properly, right?"

After hours of repetitive and fervent questioning, Marinakos seemed almost relieved at my brief line of questioning, which deflected blame from him. For the most part, I was agreeing with his assessment of what had happened because it was consistent with our theories about the role of the Salvation Army. I even called the attempts to get access to the roof "a noble effort" on the part of STB and Campbell. That was not the kind of description he had been hearing through the grueling questioning for days prior to my inquiries.

"Of course, yes," he said, agreeing with me that this was all "in the interest of safety."

There was, I asked him, "a safe way" to take that wall down. But that was contingent on getting on the roof.

"That's correct," he said.

I then asked him about his "frustration," about his concerns and dismay when "the Salvation Army didn't seem to be cooperating to give the people access to that roof to do things properly."

"Is that overall a fair characterization of what from your point of view was happening?" I asked.

"It was like two people talking across each other," he said, adding, "Yeah, I was frustrated."

When I told him I wasn't going to ask him to rehash and repeat the events of June 4, he quietly replied, "Thank you, sir."

But I had one other key question, a question that, with the right answer, would align with the heart of our case.

"Can we agree," I asked, "that if there was that level of cooperation that was given by the Salvation Army to give those people you were working with access to the roof and they had enough time to do what they wanted to do, that there was the ability to safely take down that party wall so that this collapse may have never happened? Is that overall a fair statement?"

"Potentially yes," Marinakos replied.

My colloquy with Marinakos lasted only about 10 minutes. With that, I had what I wanted from one of the key witnesses in the criminal and civil trials linked to the most catastrophic building collapse in Philadelphia history.

CHAPTER SEVEN

SEAN BENSCHOP WAS no stranger to the criminal justice system. He knew how the game was played. So he probably realized after a preliminary hearing in May 2015 that he had lost what might have been his only chance to beat the case against him.

At that pretrial hearing in the Philadelphia Common Pleas Court, a judge denied his lawyer's motion to prohibit the District Attorney from using the results of his blood test as evidence at the criminal trial. This was the test that indicated that while he was operating the excavator on the morning the wall collapsed, Benschop's blood showed traces of both marijuana and the narcotic Percocet. Strong enough traces, the DA intended to argue, that Benschop was impaired and should not have been operating a piece of heavy machinery.

Benschop's lawyer at that point, William Davis, argued that the police did not have probable cause when they asked for the blood test. What's more, the lawyer contended, his client, who was in the hospital being treated for a hand injury, had never granted permission.

Assistant District Attorney Edward Cameron, assigned to the case by DA Williams, was at the time considered one of the top homicide prosecutors in the office. Cameron, like Selber, was well seasoned and highly effective. Cameron told Judge Glenn B. Bronson that police had obtained Benschop's permission, noting that Benschop also voluntarily told them he had been taking Percocet.

Bronson, who has an excellent "no-nonsense" reputation, denied the motion to block introduction of the drug tests. He ruled that they could be used at trial. Two months later, Benschop pleaded guilty to six counts of involuntary manslaughter as well as charges of conspiracy, causing a catastrophe and reckless endangerment. Under the plea deal worked out with the DA's Office, the third-degree murder charges he faced were dropped. This was a "victory" of sorts. Under the law, anyone convicted of more than one count of third-degree murder could be sentenced to life without parole.

Instead, it appeared that Benschop was looking at from ten to twenty years in prison. What's more, there was a strong indication that he had agreed to testify for the prosecution against Griffin Campbell. Benschop would join Marinakos on the witness stand. He didn't have immunity, but his guilty plea could, in fact, make him a more credible witness.

District Attorney Seth Williams once again stepped up to provide the media with a sound bite that would lead the television and radio reports that day.

"Today's guilty plea is a substantial step in our work to fully prosecute this case," he said, "and so I'd like to take this opportunity to thank the community, SEPTA, the City of Philadelphia and all the witnesses who offered testimony and evidence that led to Mr. Benschop's plea today."

Assistant District Attorney Jennifer Selber, in response to a question from reporters, said that Benschop was "willing to cooperate" but that "we haven't made a decision yet to call him."

Everyone expected Benschop would be on the witness stand at the Griffin Campbell trial.

His cooperation and the story he would tell were part of the continuing narrative orchestrated by City Hall and the DA's Office. There was, from our perspective, never any focused intention on the part of City officials to fully prosecute all potentially responsible parties. From day one, the mayor had pointed to Campbell and Benschop. Basciano also was a potential target, but Marinakos's immunity deal had short-circuited any attempt, however feeble, to go in that direction. Moreover, no one in City government ever suggested that the Salvation Army was responsible.

That was our job.

What often got lost in all the headlines, rhetoric and posturing was the emotional toll the tragedy was continuing to take. Seven people had died, and no matter what the criminal justice system did, there was no way to make up for the hurt and loss suffered by the families of those victims. It was abundantly clear that the friends and family members of the victims who died were significantly suffering, but we also had twelve survivors who were injured, including Mariya.

And there were also the families of Benschop and Campbell.

"Sean has accepted responsibility," said Tynisha Gregory, Benschop's wife, as she left the courthouse after he entered his guilty plea. "Despite what others say, he is remorseful. He is sorry for what happened. . . . My heart goes out to the victims in this tragedy."

But when she was asked if her husband had been portrayed fairly in the media, her reply was sharp and to the point. "Hell, no," she said.

Perhaps only Kim Campbell, Griffin Campbell's wife, could fully appreciate what Tynisha Gregory was going through. Now, as a result of the guilty plea and cooperating agreement, the two women found themselves on opposite sides of the nightmare both had been living since June 5, 2013.

After the pretrial hearing back in May, Kim Campbell told reporters, "This wasn't murder, it was a terrible accident." Of her husband, she said, "He's not a monster."

At that same hearing Judge Bronson also denied a motion from Campbell's attorney, William Hobson, who wanted to use Ronald Wagenhoffer's video suicide message as evidence. The judge met with lawyers and prosecutors behind closed doors during the hearing; then when everyone returned to the courtroom, he ruled that the video could not be used. He also issued a gag order barring anyone in the case from publicizing the tape.

Wagenhoffer may have been the only City official to accept any responsibility for what had happened, but that would not be something the jury at Campbell's trial would hear. The loss and suffering of Wagenhoffer's family, however, would be part of the ongoing tragedy.

Our client, meanwhile, continued to battle for her life. Throughout 2014 and 2015, she was shuttled back and forth between the rehabilitation center and the university hospital as doctors and care workers tried to ease her pain, make her more comfortable and keep her alive.

Her dedicated children were by her side as much as possible, but because they were not citizens and were visiting on visas, they had to go back to Ukraine every six months. Oftentimes, Mariya was alone. Her attitude remained positive, and she focused on being there for them, but she also knew that she was always at risk for infection and other life-threatening illnesses. She made it through 2014 without any additional surgeries, but in March 2015 she lost her ability to speak because of the prior tracheotomies. Tracheal narrowing and collapse around the tracheostomy tube prevented her from properly exhaling through her vocal cords, thus making it impossible for her to speak. These complications have also prevented her from inhaling through her nose and mouth, and have deprived her of a sense of smell. The nasal passages are also responsible for warming and humidifying air, a process which keeps lung secretions moist and mobile. The lack of humidity in patients breathing through a tracheostomy can make their sputum become thick and sticky, which impedes their ability to clear lung secretions and leaves them susceptible to lower respiratory infections. To this day, Mariya depends on a tracheostomy to breathe and on a battery powered electro-larynx to speak (albeit with an unnatural-sounding voice).

Liz Crawford and I were frequently in touch with Mariya, and despite the number of times we saw her, she never ceased to amaze us with her resolve to survive and her ability to endure incredible amounts of suffering. And looming over all of her medical problems was the realization that, if we did not significantly prevail against the Salvation Army, she would end up with little or nothing. Her medical bills and the cost of what she knew would be care and attention for the rest of her life would prove to be astronomical.

Who would pay for them?

Our focus on the Salvation Army continued as the civil case moved slowly forward. In that regard, I set up the deposition of one of the primary witnesses for the Salvation Army, Major Charles Deitrick. At this point, during the preparation for and the taking of the key Salvation Army depositions, Liz was pregnant with her second baby, but I have never seen her work harder. It was clear that, just like me, she would let nothing get in the way of our success against the Salvation Army.

Deitrick, as expected, defended the charitable organization and the decisions that were made. He, along with other officials, offered explanations that would later be presented to the jury in the civil case. These were all parts of the picture I was trying to paint.

Deitrick, who had left college in Ohio in the 1970s to enroll in the Salvation Army's Officers Training School, was the spokesperson for the charity. Aside from being a major, he was also an ordained minister, as all officers were. He appeared to be dedicated, religious and focused on the "mission," which he didn't hesitate to explain. In sum, Deitrick was the litigation face that the Salvation Army was looking for, and he came off as a sincere and honest good guy.

"The Salvation Army is an expression of the gospel of Jesus Christ in that we reach and preach the community with the Word of God," he said in response to one of the first questions I asked him, "and helping them to understand that through our ministry of sharing what Christ did, that we meet human need without discrimination within the community in anything—any way, shape or form."

At another point early in the deposition he added, "I believe that we are about a mission of making opportunities available for people to see that they are loved and cared for."

During the deposition he acknowledged that he was in the habit of using inspirational quotes in his interactions with others. One of his favorites was from Vince Lombardi: "The measure of who we are is what we do with what we have." Another phrase he liked, although he wasn't sure where it came from, was "The only preparation for tomorrow is the right use of today."

The big question was how Deitrick would come off in front of a jury, that is, were his words empty platitudes or expressions he truly lived by? The deposition would help us find out. He got emotional when I questioned whether the charity was choosing profits over safety, a point that I tried to underscore repeatedly. He appeared genuine, someone who believed in what he was doing. But my goal was to show that he was also someone who, for whatever reason, failed to see how the tenets of caring for and protecting the less fortunate and needy—tenets that formed the bedrock of the Salvation Army's philosophy—had not come into play during the Army's business dealings with Basciano, STB and others. Ignoring the warnings and concerns expressed in the emails leading up to the collapse, and cavalierly refusing access to the roof, despite the concerns for safety that had been expressed, didn't seem to be in keeping with the Christian values the organization espoused.

Major John Cranford, another important Salvation Army witness, was also deposed. He offered a different picture of the Salvation Army bureaucracy. He appeared to be a man who enjoyed the status and power that came with rank, even if his was in reality a charitable organization with paramilitary trappings. Arrogance and hubris were two words he brought to mind. His attitude was one that I thought would be evident at trial and one that a jury would likely detect. In my view, Cranford was the kind of witness who required spontaneous, rigorous questioning in front of a jury—the more unpredictable the questions at trial, the better.

The deposition of Deitrick, the first Salvation Army representative deposed in the case, took three days. I took the lead on that deposition. We met in the offices of the law firm representing the Salvation Army in the civil litigation, Rawle & Henderson LLP, one of the oldest and most prestigious firms in the city. The offices were located at 1339 Chestnut Street, in the heart of Center City and about a block from City Hall. An original letter written by Alexander Hamilton is proudly displayed on the wall of that traditional Philadelphia law firm. The depositions took place on the sixteenth floor.

Jack Snyder from Rawle & Henderson was the lead attorney for the Salvation Army, and in a preview of what was to come, he and I clashed verbally throughout the depositions. Snyder's a damn good lawyer. I've battled with challenging ones in my time but Snyder, an alpha male like me, was particularly aggressive.

During a deposition, opposing attorneys have the right, under limited circumstances, to object to questions and also to advise their clients not to answer a particular question. Both tactics were in play during the depositions of the two Salvation Army officers. All of the jousting ends up on the record, and most disputes can eventually be resolved before trial. But the adversarial setup can also lead to personal attacks.

Among other things, while objecting to my intense line of questioning, Snyder would accuse me of being arrogant, sarcastic and misinformed. After I suggested that his face grew particularly red while he engaged in a tirade of verbal abuse, Snyder, in a fit of rage, made a sarcastic comment about the "shine" on my forehead resulting from my hair loss—a remark I actually thought was kind of funny although I didn't laugh. Many of the lawyers believed that, unlike the friendly relationship that Snyder and Mongeluzzi displayed toward each other, Snyder and Stern needed a kick-boxing ring. Yet it was clear to all involved that we enjoyed the verbal altercations. I must admit that I enjoyed witnessing Snyder's frustration in response to my unshakable efforts to blame his client for the tragedy . . . and so it went all the way through the discovery, trial and thereafter. To Snyder's credit, he believed in his client's innocence, and I respected him for that—despite the fact that he was dead wrong.

With opposing counsel, I wasn't trying to be anyone's best friend. Over the course of the months and years leading to trial, it was apparent to me that certain plaintiff lawyers were interacting with counsel for the Salvation Army as if they were friends. I saw no need to do that. What's more, I didn't believe that was advantageous for my client or for our objectives. I recognize that others would probably say I get too overzealous and harsh. Bottom line: I didn't care if Snyder liked me—it comes with the territory. I had very specific objectives to accomplish. Ultimately, the only opinions that mattered would be those of jurors yet to be chosen, and I was doing everything I could to enhance our chances of success in the courtroom.

During the Deitrick deposition, I questioned him about newspaper articles from Florida, California and New York that focused on the business side of the Salvation Army. There was, for example, an article in the *Tampa Bay Times* published in March 2011 under the headline "Salvation Army is Part Church, Part Charity, Part Business." The story pointed out that people from all walks of life donate to the charity, which in their mind is often seen as a street missionary group like the one portrayed in the highly entertaining Broadway play *Guys and Dolls*. But the reality was that the Salvation Army in Florida alone owned a $12 million headquarters, a $3 million office complex and dozens of homes in the Tampa Bay area, all part of a largely tax-exempt local real estate portfolio worth a handsome $75 million.

The story also stated that officers lived in rent-free homes, including some worth more than $300,000, and that those officers were provided with cars, health insurance, furniture, internet service and, in some cases, homeowner's association dues. At the same time, the report noted that much of the charity's financial information is kept secret because it's a church, even though it receives "hundreds of millions in tax dollars for government-funded programs it operates locally and nationwide."

A *Los Angeles Times* article from March 2010, headlined "The Salvation Army is a Residential Real Estate Powerhouse," pointed out that the charity "owns houses in Los Angeles and Orange Counties worth about $52 million" and noted that the homes were often provided to officers rent-free in lieu of higher pay.

Finally, a story in a weekly newspaper from the Upper West Side in New York City read in part, "The Salvation Army is an international faith-based organization founded in the 19th century to help the 'downtrodden, tired and poor.' In the past years, the organization has been selling several buildings in New York, including a homeless shelter in Chinatown that fetched $30 million and will become a new, upscale hotel and condo complex. The Salvation Army also emptied and sold two buildings in Gramercy Park and Murray Hill a few years ago despite protest and political opposition. The group has said in the past that they can use the money they raise from real estate for more charitable work."

Those media reports, I felt, underlined one of our key arguments. The Salvation Army was in reality a *business*, with responsibilities and obligations to its employees and customers. I bombarded Deitrick with questions about the extent of the Salvation Army's wealth, and I think a lot of lawyers in the room were surprised at how far I went in that direction.

In response to my question about the organization being a "big business," Deitrick said, "I believe we are an evangelistical church that helps millions who are victims of poverty, substance abuse, and natural disasters. And because of that kind of service, it makes us a big business."

My question and his answer set the tone for our days of verbal sparring. Jack Snyder would often try to interject himself into the middle of the fray. I did my best to ignore his bellicose behavior.

The deposition also included detailed questioning about the botched negotiations for a land swap between Basciano and the charity, with Deitrick echoing the company line that Basciano and STB couldn't be trusted, constantly changed terms and were less than credible business partners.

The emails that contained warnings relating to a potential building collapse were, of course, critical. Deitrick laid out the party-line defense position that Basciano, Simmonds and Marinakos were often disingenuous in what they said and could not be believed. To buttress this contention, Deitrick contended that the Salvation Army had granted STB access to the roof during the demolition. This assertion would be contradicted by other testimony and documentary evidence.

I spent a lot of time establishing that the Salvation Army had actually breached its own safety standards relating to the Thrift Store, a line of conduct which played a substantial role in the catastrophic outcome. Specifically, I questioned Deitrick about the Salvation Army employee manual that emphasized that workers should immediately point out any problems to supervisors. The chain of command was very important in this regard. But from where I stood, it seemed to work only one way, from bottom to top. The safety manual stated that potential safety hazards should be reported *up* the chain of command, but nothing in the written policies required Salvation Army upper management to report potential safety hazards *down* the chain of command. Even though it was not in writing, I got Deitrick to admit that the upper management nonetheless had an obligation to report potential safety hazards to the employees and ultimately to the customers. I purposely put Major Deitrick in a quandary: he had to acknowledge that, although the rule was not in writing, the Salvation Army does follow a policy of reporting potential safety hazards to the store level. However, Deitrick attempted to justify the Salvation Army's decision not to report the email warnings to store employees because the threats were mere "hyperbole" and not credible.

I continued with persistent questioning, and I pointed out that the Salvation Army's own policies stated that *potential* safety hazards had to be addressed and evaluated. In other words, potential safety hazards did not have to be *verified* before employees were notified. The bottom line was that Deitrick and other Salvation Army witnesses were never able to establish that they properly investigated the potential safety hazards identified in the series of emails sent before the collapse. They were also never able to establish that they alerted store employees or customers about these potential hazards. Most important, the Salvation Army was never able to establish that it ever intended to temporarily close the store until it knew for certain that things were safe. Not only were these inexcusable failures substandard in the retail industry, but this reckless and intentional decision making also violated the Salvation Army's own safety policies!

Although all the defendants in this case would maintain that the building was not structurally dangerous until June, when the excavator was used by Sean Benschop, that defense missed the mark. As a preliminary matter, would a jury really have difficulty believing that when you demolish a dilapidated four-story building in Center City, next door to a one-story thrift store, the process is not potentially dangerous? How could this benevolent organization, one that supposedly values human life, take the position that it was appropriate to turn a blind eye to warnings? From my viewpoint, this was an indefensible position, especially in light of the Salvation Army's non-delegable duty under its own policies and the law to protect its customers and employees from potential dangers. In sum, after Deitrick's deposition, we had constructed a pivotal case theme and theory against the Salvation Army, which was, unlike its Thrift Store, indestructible.

I ended my questioning by showing Major Deitrick a terrifying picture taken during the rescue operation. It was a photograph of Mariya Plekan trapped in the rubble as rescue workers frantically tried to dig her out late at night.

When shown the photo, Deitrick said, "I see the top half of a lady, yes." I then asked that the picture be enlarged and asked if he knew who it was. He said he did not.

"Would it surprise you if I told you that's my client?" I asked.

"I'm sure you wanted me to see that that's your client, but I didn't know that," he replied.

I asked if he had ever seen the picture before, and he said he hadn't.

"You do know," I said, "she was buried alive under that rubble for thirteen hours."

"I do know that," he said.

"You do know that as a result of the crush injuries and other things that have happened to her, she's had literally half her body amputated; are you aware of that?"

"I am aware of that."

"Are you aware that she's, she's my age?" I asked. "She's going to have a normal life expectancy; are you aware of that? . . . She's going to live that way the rest of her life?"

I then asked Liz to call up another picture on the video screen, a picture of the Salvation Army motto "Doing the Most Good," which is prominently displayed at the top of its national website and frequently appears in other Army publications and notices. It's a phrase, like the Lombardi quote, designed to encourage and inspire.

"You've seen that quote before, haven't you, sir?" I asked.

"I have," Deitrick replied.

"Did the Salvation Army do the most good for her?" I asked, nodding toward the photo of my client trapped in the rubble.

"Salvation Army did all we could to protect her," he said.

That, of course, was the issue at the heart of the litigation.

"We'll let the jury decide that," I said.

CHAPTER EIGHT

GRIFFIN CAMPBELL said he had a plan to take the wall down safely.

He just needed access to the Thrift Store roof. After all, he had successfully taken down the other nearby buildings without incident before working on the Hoagie City structure.

"I thought it would be the safest way to just put a ladder on the roof, one man up on the ladder with a hammer and chisel," he said. "It's a much longer process, but hammer and chisel and knock it in one brick at a time, and when you're knocking it one brick at a time, you're not knocking in these massive pieces that you had to pull in toward you. So that was the decision I made to go on the roof and knock it in one brick at a time."

But despite promises, he said, he never got permission to get on the roof from the Salvation Army, and he was never in the loop—never part of the emails, phone calls and memos that dealt with the access issue.

That's the story Campbell told when he took the witness stand in his own defense at his criminal trial in Common Pleas Court. For several hours over two days in October 2015, the burly construction company owner tried to explain to a jury what had happened at 22nd and Market Streets on June 5, 2013, and why he was not responsible for the tragedy. From the witness stand, Campbell disputed the stories offered earlier in the trial by Plato Marinakos and Sean Benschop. Both men, he implied, were lying or distorting the facts.

We monitored the trial because the testimony and evidence would be highly relevant to the civil litigation that was pending and because our client, Mariya Plekan, was going to testify. It was important to understand where three principal figures—Campbell, Benschop and Marinakos—stood. Finger-pointing, fixing blame and shifting responsibility were all part of the game. We had to be able to sift through it all while staying focused on our client's primary objective. What quickly became apparent was that some of the other plaintiffs had differing objectives.

Access to the roof would always be one of the key issues. Whether Campbell was criminally liable or merely incompetent in the way he went about his business was a secondary matter for our purposes. The District Attorney's Office, of course, had a different approach. Sounding the theme that the City adopted from day one, prosecutors argued that Campbell was at the "center of culpability."

"It's money over lives," Assistant District Attorney Jennifer Selber told the jury of seven women and five men in her opening statement. "What do you say to a person who makes those kinds of choices? You say guilty."

Campbell, she said, was someone who had readily and knowingly cut corners to maximize his profits, winning the job with a low-bid offer that almost guaranteed safety would not be a primary issue.

William Hobson, Campbell's attorney, called his client a "fall guy" in a tragedy that had rocked the city and that had officials tripping over one another in a rush to judgment. He said his client was "not a murderer," but rather a scapegoat who had been betrayed by a man he thought was his friend, Plato Marinakos Jr. Marinakos, Hobson said, was a "weasel and a Judas."

The District Attorney's Office set the stage for what would be a thirteen-day trial by calling Philadelphia Police Detective Paul Guercio as its first witness. Guercio was one of the first on the scene, responding to a radio call while driving in his car near the site.

"I rounded the corner and that's when I saw it," the veteran police officer said. "Oh my God, it was apocalyptic."

He said he jumped out of his car and ran toward the rubble.

"I ran onto the pile and tried to help people," he told the jury. "You could hear 'Help me' [from some victims], but you didn't know where they were."

Setting the scene of death and destruction, the prosecution used photos and video to give the jury an eyewitness view of what had happened. A scale model of the block of Market Street and the buildings, set at one-thirty-second of actual size, was frequently referenced as prosecutors took witnesses through the events of the day.

Guercio said the Thrift Store had been "pancaked" by the wall that collapsed on it, and he described the "utter chaos" that first responders found at the scene. He said he remained at the site until about 2 a.m. He was there when the bodies were recovered and when Mariya Plekan was miraculously rescued late that night. The jury, somber and focused, took it all in as Guercio's testimony gave names to the bodies and provided other details about the rescue and recovery operation that was depicted on screen in the third-floor courtroom of the Criminal Justice Center.

Family members of several of the victims were in the courtroom, including Nancy Winkler and her husband, Jay Bryan. In a compelling news report that succinctly captured the moment, veteran *Philadelphia Inquirer* court reporter Joe Slobodzian wrote that they (understandably) "looked away when the photo of the young woman covered in dust and curled in a fetal position appeared on screen."

Griffin Campbell, sitting quietly at the defense table, was pointed to by the DA as the man responsible for the carnage.

The videos, the photos and the eyewitness testimony laid the groundwork for that argument. Our client, Mariya Plekan, was used to drive the point home. It was her first court appearance, although she had given her trial deposition in the civil case and had been interviewed on camera for a television news report that marked the first anniversary of the collapse. She was starting to emerge as the face of the tragedy; she was the victim whose suffering could be put in front of a jury, the living example of everything that had gone wrong that day. Unfortunately, for whatever reason, she was the silent victim—the papers continued to focus principally on the tragic deaths, leaving out the most catastrophically injured survivor.

Mariya was on the witness stand for about forty minutes, again recounting the horror, the fear and the anxiety of being buried alive for more than thirteen hours. Speaking through an interpreter, she told the jury that she thought she was going to die that day, pinned under the rubble, barely able to move and in mental anguish as her cries for help went unanswered. As Liz and I sat in court riveted to her every word, we didn't know this would be Mariya's last court appearance before she permanently lost her ability to speak. In the future, she would have to rely on a reverberating throat device to help her communicate.

"I lost hope . . . that anyone would ever find me," she said, before recounting the miraculous rescue. She said the man—Fire Captain John O'Neill—and the dog were so close she could feel the dog's breath as he sniffed through the debris. She screamed for help and heard O'Neill shout, "There's a living person here!"

The rescue, she said, freed her from the rubble, but not from her suffering.

"This is my hell," she said of the wheelchair-bound existence she now endures, the loss of the lower half of her body, the more than thirty operations she has endured.

Without her children, she said, "I would have lost my mind." Her struggle was always about her children and her grandchild. That's what kept her strong and gave her the will to live. She never wavered.

Her testimony was used to end the prosecution's presentation to the jury. Although her voice was artificially modulated by her handheld throat device, Mariya added a human voice and real emotion to a case that had largely been built around the finger-pointing of the DA's two key witnesses.

Sean Benschop and Plato Marinakos had testified before her. Their stories were consistent with their earlier statements. Benschop said he was just taking orders from Campbell. Marinakos, relying on the catch phrase that defined his every appearance under oath, insisted that Campbell was in charge of the "means and methods" of demolition.

"I was to monitor the progress of the demolition so the owner would know when to pay him," he said in response to a question from Assistant District Attorney Edward Cameron, who was assigned to try the case along with Selber. Marinakos also claimed that if Campbell had said the work in progress was "unsafe," he would have said, "Let's stop the job immediately."

This assertion, of course, begged a question that was never asked. What about the emails warning of the danger that dominated the correspondence between STB and the Salvation Army in the weeks leading up to the tragedy? Wasn't other parties' knowledge of a dangerous condition, to which Campbell and Benschop were not privy, relevant as to potential criminal intent? Marinakos, executives with STB, officials with the Salvation Army and a deputy mayor and his top assistant were privy to those emails. Yet no one stepped forward and said, "Let's stop the job immediately."

The District Attorney appeared reluctant to pursue that line of questioning in the criminal investigation. Marinakos, of course, had been given immunity in exchange for his testimony. Basciano had sought refuge behind his Fifth Amendment rights against self-incrimination and had not been called to testify. And only Campbell's lawyer, in what proved to be a futile exercise, tried to introduce the idea that the Salvation Army might share in the blame.

All of that left the jury with a less than complete and perhaps distorted picture of the how and why behind the collapse. Campbell's testimony further clouded that picture. He insisted that Marinakos had never told him on June 4, 2013, that the wall had to come down immediately. He also said he never would have suggested erecting scaffolding to get the job done, as Marinakos had asserted.

"It's impossible," Campbell said in response to a question from his lawyer. "[D]ebris from the top two floors [that had been gutted earlier] were in that hole and the only way you can move—I would have to hire fifty men to move the debris. The debris, it could probably only be moved by a machine operator. No way men could have moved the debris, erect scaffolding up. . . ."

Throughout his testimony, Campbell said Marinakos had promised to guide him through the demolition project. That, he said, was the only reason he bid on the job; that and the promise of more work once the demolition was completed and Basciano's grandiose "Gateway" project was launched.

"I got the signal loud and clear from Plato," he said, "that once we get through this project that I would never have any money problems again."

Campbell said his demolition experience was limited, but Marinakos had promised to be with him every step of the way.

"He agreed to help, that's the reason I took the job," he told the jury. "The reason I took the job was the promise of the future and that he was going to help me take this building down."

The means and methods, Campbell said in so many words, were not his responsibility. That was on Marinakos.

"Plato directed me how to take the building down," he said at one point. At another point he told the jury, "He was guiding me through the demolition."

When asked by his lawyer if he did what Plato told him to do, Campbell replied, "Of course. He paid me."

Money was a constant issue during Campbell's testimony.

He disputed what had become one of the persistent arguments from investigators—that salvaging the beams and joists had created the instability and that the income from that salvaged material was what drove Campbell to cut corners and create a less than stable situation.

Campbell acknowledged that he had made between $20,000 and $25,000 from salvaged material taken from the job site. But he said he had salvaged less than three hundred of the twenty-seven hundred joists that came out of the buildings during the demolition.

"On the joists I might have made three or four thousand [dollars]," he said. "The money I made wasn't really in the joists. It was in the copper, the wiring. . . . That's where I made money."

Money was also at the heart of a discussion about what his lawyer called "kickbacks" to Marinakos, although the judge upheld a prosecution objection to the use of that specific word. Campbell, who said he had been doing business with Marinakos for a few years, frankly admitted that he gave the architect cash from time to time, an allegation Marinakos has continually denied. Campbell said it was just a way things were done.

"You got to understand that each deal he made for me, he probably made room for his self to get something," he explained. "He's not going to keep giving me deals and not getting anything."

Asked if he thought that was wrong, Campbell replied. "No, it's done all the time."

Campbell also challenged Benschop's account of the events leading up to the collapse of the wall. He said Benschop was supposed to be using the excavator that morning to lift and place heavy debris in a dumpster, not chip away at the eastern wall, as Benschop had testified. He also said that, had he known Benschop had smoked a joint that morning, he would not have allowed him to work.

"If I know anyone on my job site was smoking marijuana, they wouldn't be working on my job site," he said.

Campbell insisted he had done nothing wrong, that he was just trying to do a job, to earn a living. And he said for a second time that he knew how to take the wall down safely. What's more, he said, Marinakos agreed.

"The safest way I thought, and Plato thought, would be, is put the two men on a ladder and let them chip it in one piece at a time," he said. "He's telling me we're going to figure out how to get you on the roof . . . so just take your time and do this. There never was a time limit on getting the job done. Take your time. Let your men chisel the wall down and everything will be all right."

But that never happened. Instead, Campbell said, he ended up in jail, accused of murder.

"I would have shoveled horse manure before I put anyone's life in danger," he told the jury "I didn't kill anybody. I didn't intend to hurt anybody. I got up and I went to work."

The jury also heard from two Salvation Army workers, Margarita Agosto, the manager of the Thrift Store, and Ralph Pomponi, the regional supervisor to whom Agosto reported. Both were called by the defense. Both acknowledged that Campbell had asked for access to the roof. Both said they were not in a position to grant it.

Agosto, a thirty-nine-year-old mother of six, had worked on and off for the Salvation Army for several years. She became the manager of the Thrift Store at 22nd and Market in February 2013. She had been deposed in our civil litigation in April and had also been questioned under oath in the OSHA investigation. Her testimony at the criminal trial was limited, focused primarily on Campbell's request to get on the roof. She said she had referred him to Pomponi.

Margarita Agosto had been injured but survived the collapse. Her more detailed account of what had happened and the events leading up to it had emerged during two days of depositions back in April, and her story would figure prominently in the pending civil litigation. Liz and I saw her as an important witness who would help make our case much stronger against the Salvation Army. We were also sympathetic to the fact that she was just trying to make a living and provide for her children. Others, including some plaintiff attorneys and lawyers for the Salvation Army, took a different approach.

In fact, the Salvation Army tried to scapegoat her, implying that she had authority to close the store but opted not to, even though she had knowledge of potential dangers. From my perspective, the weight of the evidence indicated that was a falsehood. It was clear she was relying on her supervisor, Ralph Pomponi, to make the decision. While we attempted to support and buttress her testimony, which directly conflicted with Pomponi's, other lawyers saw her as "SA management" and at the civil trial attempted to lump her in the group that was responsible and accountable for what had happened. After all, reasoned certain plaintiff lawyers, if Agosto is part of SA management and the jury is critical of Agosto, we can prevail against SA on that theory alone. I recognized the legal logic behind this argument, but I truly believed that Agosto was telling the truth.

All of that, of course, was down the road. Her court appearance in Campbell's criminal trial was just a preliminary. But the story Agosto and Pomponi outlined before the jury in the criminal case offered a ground-level look inside the tragedy.

Pomponi said he met once with Campbell, but said he was not able to give him permission for access to the Thrift Store roof. "I told him that I couldn't authorize that," Pomponi said, describing a meeting with Campbell in either April or May 2013. "So he gave me a card with his name on it, and I told him I would forward it to my supervisor."

Pomponi said that's what he did. His supervisor? Major John Cranford.

Campbell's attorney ended his cross-examination of Pomponi with this question: "As the district manager responsible for the safety of your employees and the customers you invite to that store, do you believe that the Salvation Army shares responsibility in the accident?"

Before Pomponi could answer, Assistant District Attorney Jennifer Selber objected. Judge Glenn B. Bronson sustained the objection.

"Ridiculous," Selber said of Hobson's question.

"Nothing further," said Hobson.

"I object to him asking questions that he knows full well are objectionable," Selber added.

"Sit down, okay," the judge told the Assistant District Attorney. "Just state the grounds for your objection. There's no reason to make a speech."

Bronson had told the jury that its only responsibility was to weigh the evidence against Griffin Campbell. The jury should not concern itself, he said, with whether anyone else should have been charged or might have been responsible. In that light, Hobson's question may not have been legally relevant to the criminal charges that Campbell faced, but it certainly went to the heart of our civil litigation.

One other minor point, not brought out at the criminal trial, said a lot about the players in this tragedy. It had to do with Pomponi's visit to the store, even though he and Agosto disagreed on the precise date.

Pomponi had said he was in the store the day before the wall collapsed.

Agosto, in a deposition in our civil case, said she thought it might have been a few days, possibly a week, earlier. Whatever day it was,

Agosto had expressed concern about the demolition work going on, and the rumbling and the debris falling on the roof and down the inside of the wall of the Thrift Store.

"I covered my head and said, 'Oh my God, it's going to fall,'" she said.

"Don't worry about it," she said Pomponi told her. "It's okay. You're all right."

She said he told her "nothing was going to happen."

In fairness, Pomponi was probably not aware of the emails and warnings. But if, as he said, he was at the store on June 4, it would have been hard to miss the demolition taking place next door or the free-standing, unbraced wall that hovered over the Salvation Army Thrift Store.

The reason for his visit that morning added another twist. He had come to repair or replace a cash register that wasn't working. Taking care of the cash register was a priority. The Salvation Army wanted to make certain the flow of money into the Thrift Store would be properly monitored and recorded. It cared less, we would argue, about the safety of those who came to buy and those whose job it was to sell.

The jury got the criminal case late on a Friday afternoon, October 16, and deliberated briefly before being sent home for the weekend. The panel returned Monday morning and reached a verdict shortly after noon. In all, deliberations lasted about five hours.

Griffin Campbell was found guilty of six counts of involuntary manslaughter and thirteen counts of reckless endangerment. He was also found guilty of aggravated assault and causing a catastrophe. But the jury found him not guilty of third-degree murder and conspiracy. The third-degree murder charges could have resulted in a life sentence. But a conviction on those charges required a jury to determine he had acted with malice.

The judge set January 8, 2016, as the sentencing date for both Campbell and Benschop. Both men remained in jail.

District Attorney Seth Williams, as always, was quick with a sound bite for the media.

"No verdict can replace the lives that were lost that June morning," he said, "but I hope today's verdict brings more closure and healing to the friends and families of those who were injured and lost their lives."

He then added that the verdicts were a "powerful reminder that jobsite safety is paramount and if someone breaks the law . . . they will be punished to the fullest extent of the law."

William Hobson, Campbell's lawyer, told members of the media that it had been a tough battle. He said the deaths and destruction were "a human tragedy that will forever be etched in the minds of the city. . . . Let's hope this is the end of it."

For those of us involved in the civil litigation, it was just the beginning.

CHAPTER NINE

GRIFFIN CAMPBELL'S conviction was the headline, but the real story was our preparation for the civil trial. We believed that's where justice would be served, although it became clear rather quickly that not all the lawyers on our side of the case shared the strategy we had mapped to get there.

We—Liz Crawford and I—continued to be the only attorneys completely focused on the Salvation Army as we approached trial. Our goal was to show that the tragedy could have been avoided, would have been avoided, were it not for a combination of misinformation and faulty assumptions steeped in arrogance and hubris. Our strategy was to show that from February 2013, when Marinakos first sent the letter raising questions about the poor condition of the Salvation Army Thrift Store building, through June 5, when the wall collapsed, upper management with the Army viewed every question, every complaint and every warning as an attempt by STB to take advantage of the situation. We wanted to show that practically every Salvation Army decision, including decisions to take no action, was driven by financial rather than safety concerns. It was all there in the depositions we took in the run-up to the civil trial, which was set to begin in September 2016. Our objective was to take that information and fashion it into a narrative that would show a civil jury how and why the tragedy had happened and, most important, how it could have been avoided. The other plaintiff lawyers liked this approach and assisted in the overall prosecution of the case against the Salvation Army; however, they were reluctant to focus solely on the Salvation Army as the primary target in court.

Our position would always be that the Salvation Army was a catalyst for the "apocalyptic" events of June 5, 2013, and was in the best position to protect people. The Salvation Army, we believed, was not a victim of those events but rather their principal cause.

The first hurdle we faced was a result of a judge's decision, in response to a defense motion, to bifurcate the litigation. This meant that the first phase of the trial would focus only on liability—who was responsible and to what degree. If we prevailed in that phase of the trial, then there would be a second phase focusing on damages—how much those who had been found liable should pay.

In theory, the bifurcation would allow the jury to objectively analyze the evidence without being swayed by the emotional tug of death, maiming and destruction that was so much a part of the story. But bifurcation made it more difficult to support our claim against the Salvation Army. The collapse of the wall could easily be linked to the demolition work. And that attached liability up the ladder from Griffin Campbell to Plato Marinakos to Richard Basciano and his company, STB. We had to show how and why the Salvation Army, which always portrayed itself as another victim, was responsible and explain why it should substantially share in the liability for what happened.

We had arguments that related to two key claims of intentional misconduct: "intentional infliction of emotional distress" and "extreme and outrageous conduct." In the first phase of the trial, we needed to convince the jury that the Salvation Army's actions supported both those allegations. As a matter of law, if the jury found the Salvation Army liable for claims involving *intentional* misconduct, the Salvation Army would have to pay the full monetary amount of the verdict without contribution from other potentially responsible parties. Regarding our claims of *negligence*, the jury had to find the Salvation Army at least sixty percent responsible for us to achieve our goal; at that level of responsibility, the Army would have to satisfy the entire monetary amount of the verdict regardless of another party's ability to pay. Most of the plaintiffs' lawyers refused to believe it was possible for a jury to find the Salvation Army sixty percent or more responsible, and this explained why they chose to spread the blame at trial in order to maintain their credibility with the jury.

Liz and I took the direct approach of primarily blaming the Army. We argued that the Army had kept the store open despite the repeated and ever more frantic warnings from people like Marinakos and STB official Thomas Simmonds and that the Army had repeatedly denied Campbell and STB access to the roof. The access question was crucial from our viewpoint. The emails and memos were all about access. Indeed, the owner's representatives had used the email warnings in an effort to convince the Salvation Army that access to the Thrift Store was critical. We had to get those facts and the Salvation Army's cavalier and arbitrary denial of access in front of a jury during the first phase of the trial.

Many of the other plaintiff attorneys expressed grave concerns about what might be perceived by the jury as an assault on the Salvation Army, a reputable and well-known charity. But I was convinced it was the linchpin of the litigation. We had to show that we weren't suing a charity, but rather a business, an international business with a net worth of over $10 billion. In fact, at one point Major Deitrick had put the Army's total value at more than $14 billion. So throughout the entire deposition process I looked for testimony that would support our position: that by opening for business that morning—given everything it knew—the Salvation Army was the key player in the liability.

Major Cranford, when he was deposed in March 2015, spoke directly to that point. He was skillfully questioned by Steven Wigrizer, who represented two of the women who had died in the collapse: Roseline Conteh, the fifty-two-year old nursing assistant and immigrant from Sierra Leone who was shopping in the store that morning, and Mary Simpson, the twenty-four-year-old who was bargain hunting with her friend Anne Bryan, who also perished. During the discovery phase, we had agreed that the work would be spread around, so Steve led off with Cranford and I got Deitrick. In fact, the decision-making regarding who took which deposition was essentially a group process, subject to a majority vote in the event of a disagreement.

Major Cranford acknowledged under oath that he had read all the warning emails Thomas Simmonds had sent, but never acted on them. Nor, he said, did he ever inform anyone at the store or in the field about the concerns STB was expressing. He said he never saw the need to inform Margarita Agosto, the store manager, Richard Stasiorowski, the assistant manager, or Ralph Pomponi, the field supervisor.

Pressed by Wigrizer, Cranford said it wasn't forgetfulness or inadvertence on his part, but rather a willful decision not to share that information with those under him.

He said he didn't feel they needed to know.

The same line of questioning focused on the letter in which Plato Marinakos cited the deplorable and deteriorating condition of the Thrift Store and warned about dangers posed by the demolition next door.

Cranford's response to that letter was to bring in a company that was essentially a paint and wallpaper outfit to assess the damages the demolition might cause to the property, rather than a competent structural engineer, who would have been able to analyze the possible risk to life and limb the project posed.

Cranford dismissed the Marinakos letter, saying he didn't believe most of what the architect said. Part of the backstory to this, of course, was the failed negotiations between Richard Basciano and the Salvation Army over a potential swap of properties. Cranford and other Salvation Army officials appeared to dismiss the email warnings as a negotiating tactic aimed at getting the swap of property back on the table.

Again, money drove the process. Every issue was evaluated from a financial perspective. Employees and customers were not in the loop, Cranford said, because there was no need for them to be.

Here's how part of the deposition on that issue played out:

WIGRIZER: Now, if Mr. Stasiorowski and Ms. Agosto were in that building on a daily basis, and an architect took the position that, from a structural point of view, the building they were working in was barely sound, why would not—these individuals not need to know about this conclusion?

CRANFORD: Because I believe that statement not to be true.

WIGRIZER: But wouldn't they have the right, or shouldn't they have the right to make their own judgment about that?

CRANFORD: No.

WIGRIZER: Why not?

CRANFORD: It's not their—it's not their business; it's ours.

It's not their business. That's what it came down to. They were workers, employees. They had no need to know. Business trumped safety. That's the point we wanted to make to the jury, and Cranford's statement (and overall demeanor) helped us get there.

Another witness, who was highly underrated yet proved important, was Edward Strudwick. Adam Grutzmacher, a younger lawyer who represented the estate of Kimberly Finnegan in the litigation, handled his deposition. Adam elicited some very helpful testimony from Strudwick in this discovery deposition that was not fully appreciated by the plaintiff lawyers, including me, until we were near the start of trial. Ed Strudwick was employed by the Salvation Army as a truck dispatcher after being in rehabilitation for alcohol addiction. He left the Salvation Army on good terms and had absolutely no dog in this fight. He was not a victim of the collapse, and the Salvation Army had done right by him. However, he did attend the monthly Salvation Army production meetings, including the critical May 22 meeting, about two weeks before the collapse. The minutes kept by the Salvation Army from that meeting clearly reflected a recognition of safety concerns relating to demolition.

While Major Cranford maintained that discussions regarding safety issues did not take place at that meeting, Ed Strudwick painted a different picture of the meeting and of Major Cranford's demeanor. Strudwick testified that Mrs. Cranford brought up the possibility of closing or at least temporarily relocating the store while demolition was underway. The meeting notes indicate that Major Cranford shut down that discussion. Strudwick also said Major Cranford was adamant about denying STB access to "his roof." Strudwick's testimony made Major Cranford sound like a dictator, implying his store's business was more important than the safety of his customers or employees (or his wife's genuine concerns). When trial came, other plaintiffs' lawyers disagreed with my decision to bring Strudwick to the stand, in part because of his admitted ongoing battle with alcoholism, and also because we heard that he had recently experienced a disfiguring infection on his face. But I felt strongly that he would be the only objective witness in this case who could allow the jury to see another side of the Salvation Army. In sum, Strudwick's impressions would undermine the Army's lofty and holy stature.

We also planned to use the Salvation Army employee manual itself to underline the safety issue. "The safety and security of our customers, beneficiaries and employees is one of our most important concerns," the manual reads. We would argue that, based on its own manual, the Army's failure to take action—instead turning a blind eye—constituted "extreme and outrageous conduct." The words of Salvation Army officials during the deposition process helped bolster that contention. Deitrick and Cranford, the two Salvation Army majors, gave us part of what we wanted, but for an emotional, ground-level account, we needed more. We needed the words of someone who was there.

We needed Margarita Agosto.

The hard-working, thirty-nine-year-old mother of six had quit her job with the Salvation Army after the accident and eventually received a workers' comp settlement. She, like all employees, was prohibited by law from bringing suit against the Army. But she had filed against STB, Basciano and Marinakos. Her lawyer, Jerome Gamburg, worked with us in preparing his client for both the deposition and trial testimony. Jerome had been practicing law longer than any of the other plaintiff lawyers in the case. He is also a gentleman and a straight shooter.

His client was deposed on April 22, 2015, in the Rawle & Henderson Law Office. By that point it was already becoming clear that some, if not all, of the defendants intended to argue that Agosto, as the Salvation Army store manager on the scene, had the authority and obligation to close the store. Agosto also knew that Ralph Pomponi, her supervisor, was denying that she had ever raised concerns to him about the demolition.

Pomponi in many ways emerged as the same kind of legal buffer for the Salvation Army that Marinakos, through his grant of immunity, had provided for Basciano and STB in the criminal investigation. Pomponi was deposed in January 2015, several months before Agosto.

Among other things, Pomponi said that, had Agosto told him of her concerns that the building might collapse, "I would have notified my supervisor." And he insisted that his supervisor, Major Cranford, would have taken action to deal with the problem.

"There's no doubt in my mind," Pomponi said.

Pomponi said he was in the store the day before the collapse, which conflicted somewhat with Agosto's recollection that he was there about a week before. And he said for a second time, "If she had told me that day, I would have notified my supervisor."

Pomponi acknowledged that he had not been told about the prior warnings that Cranford and the others had received. And he said he was not aware of what would emerge as a key element in the Salvation Army's defense. Cranford and the other officials had argued that they believed STB had agreed to halt all demolition until the roof access question was resolved. This position seemed to fly in the face of the facts and was somewhat disingenuous, given the memos and testimony indicating Cranford had no intention of ever allowing roof access. Indeed, Strudwick's testimony was clear that Cranford was adamantly opposed to access altogether.

For us, this was another example of misinformation, miscalculation, arrogance and hubris on the part of the Salvation Army.

Admittedly, Pomponi may have been in the dark about the "understanding" that no demolition was to take place until the access issue was resolved. And that may have been the reason he hadn't reacted to the demolition and to the unbraced wall hovering over the Thrift Store on the day he visited. He said that if he had known that the Salvation Army believed no demolition was taking place, he would have informed Cranford that work, in fact, was being done. That being said, he also insisted that he did not see the extent of the demolition or the wall looming over the store. In an explanation that stretched credulity, he said that he drove to the store the day before the collapse by way of the South Street exit on the Schuylkill Expressway. This route would have taken him about sixteen blocks out of his way, but it meant that he didn't drive up Market Street past the demolition project. Mongeluzzi's persistent questioning on this point was particularly effective and helped to successfully attack Pomponi's credibility.

"That's just the route I took," Pomponi said when asked about the circuitous driving pattern.

And when he left the store that morning, he insisted, he never looked to his right, but rather looked left as he pulled out into traffic on Market Street, thus again missing a chance to view the demolition in progress and the unbraced wall.

There was, on the other hand, nothing circuitous about the testimony of Margarita Agosto, who, in response to one of my questions, frankly said that, had she been made aware of all the warnings and concerns expressed about the demolition work, "I wouldn't even [have] come to work" on June 5.

Dressed in a green sweater over a white shirt and wearing black-rimmed glasses, Ms. Agosto looked like a librarian as she detailed the events leading up to the tragedy and the role she had played in them.

She said she had always believed that her superiors at the Salvation Army would look out for her, her workers and her customers. And she thought that anyone doing a demolition job in the heart of the city would have the expertise and experience to do it correctly.

Both those opinions changed, she said, in the aftermath of the collapse.

"Toward the end, like I seen the wall standing there," she said in response to a question I asked, "but I didn't . . . I'm not a construction worker. I don't know. In my head I'm thinking, okay, they know what they're doing. They're professionals."

She again repeated that Pomponi had assured her there was nothing to worry about, adding, "his being my boss, I figured he also has my best interests and my workers' best interests. So I didn't say nothing after that. . . . It was my thinking that, okay, if they knew what was going on or that if they haven't come to me and said, 'Well, you know what, let's close the store,' then I figured, okay, we're fine. They have their best interests for me. They're my boss."

When I told her that some were now suggesting she didn't care and could have closed the store, she shot back, "They should have come to me and said, 'What do you think? Is it safe?'"

But those were two questions no one in authority with the Salvation Army wanted to ask. Or, from the view expressed by Major Cranford, saw the need to ask.

Agosto said she had just finished arranging some items in the store that morning and was working on a cart when what seemed like a "smoke and wind" storm blasted through the building. After that, she said, came the chaos, the screaming and yelling, the calls for help. She was hit on the head with something that fell from the ceiling, but managed to scramble to safety. She said she found Richard Stasiorowski, her assistant manager, and they began counting heads, trying to determine who had gotten out and who might still be inside.

Kimberly Finnegan, working the cash register her first day on the job, hadn't made it, she said sadly; neither had the avuncular and always smiling Borbor Davis, who had been sorting clothes in the basement.

Nearly two years after the tragedy, Margarita Agosto said, she still was haunted by the events that day. When I asked if she had recovered from her injuries, she said, "Physically, yes. Mentally, no."

Her story was essentially consistent with testimony she had given during the OSHA investigation. During that probe, she had recounted how she and other workers would nervously joke about the noise and the shaking and the debris that landed on the roof and seemed to be coming down inside the walls.

"Oh my God, imagine if this falls on us," she said in her OSHA statement. "We would say that, but we were clueless . . . we didn't really know what was going on."

And the point I wanted to drive home during her deposition is that no one in authority with the Salvation Army saw any need to tell her or the people who worked under her at the store what was going on.

Yet defense attorneys for the Salvation Army and STB continued to argue that she should have closed the store.

"I don't have the right to close any stores down," she said when I asked her about this. "I don't have the right to say anything. The only thing that I had the responsibility to do is to make sure that my chain of command know what's going on, and I did."

June 5, 2013, she said, "was a day that shouldn't have happened."

Looking back and knowing what she did now, I asked, if she had had the authority, would she have closed the store?

"Absolutely," she said.

Asked that same question so many times and in so many different ways, no one with authority within the Salvation Army would offer what to me seemed like the only logical and sensible response—the response that Margarita Agosto offered without hesitation.

It was clear that upper-level management with the Salvation Army, including principally Cranford, was in a position to close the store. They knew of the warnings, yet refused to do anything.

I also took the deposition of Major Kevin Schoch, who was Major Cranford's successor when Cranford left for retirement Schoch said he was aware of at least two different occasions when the Salvation Army had closed its thrift stores for safety reasons. One store was in the Torresdale section of Philadelphia. The other was the Thrift Store in Atlantic City, which was shuttered for a few days in the wake of Hurricane Sandy. Documents and memos from the Salvation Army indicated there was some internal debate over whether the Atlantic City store should have been closed. Regardless, Schoch's testimony was a missing link that helped us establish other instances where the Salvation Army had knowledge of safety concerns and decided to close a store.

Like the store at 22nd and Market Streets, the Atlantic City store was a major revenue generator. But in that case, it seemed, safety trumped profits.

On January 8, 2016, Griffin Campbell was sentenced to fifteen to thirty years in prison. Sean Benschop, in light of his guilty plea and agreement to cooperate, got half that time. As of this writing, both men are still in jail.

During the sentencing hearing, Benschop expressed his remorse and said he should have walked away from the project rather than firing up the excavator that morning. He sobbed as he told Judge Glenn Bronson that he had become friendly with one of the victims, Borbor Davis. The two men were both immigrants, Benschop from Guyana and Davis from Liberia. They would often talk while taking coffee breaks, standing along Ludlow Street, which ran parallel to Market Street behind the Thrift Store and the buildings Benschop was helping Campbell demolish.

"When I learned he was dead . . . I couldn't believe it," Benschop told the judge.

While Benschop expressed remorse, Griffin Campbell continued to insist that he had done nothing wrong, rehashing the arguments he and his lawyer had made during the trial. He never intended to hurt anyone and was only trying to earn an honest living, he said.

"This job meant a lot to me, a lot," he said. "I was going to be out of debt and life was going to be good." He asked Bronson for a "fair chance to prove to you, your honor, the person that I am."

But the jury had already decided that issue based on the evidence presented in that courtroom.

"There is no adequate way to describe here the impact of this on the victims and the many victims who did not die," Bronson said while imposing sentence on Campbell. "This tragedy shocked this city to its core. We may never feel quite the same walking down the streets of Center City Philadelphia."

Those who had perished, the judge said, "suffered a terrible death, buried alive, suffocating."

Campbell's lawyer, as he had done during the trial, made emotional arguments that his client was a scapegoat and that there were racial overtones to the prosecution. He pointed out that the only two people charged criminally were black, while the white property owner (Basciano) and the white architect (Marinakos) were not held accountable.

The prosecution continued to insist that there was never enough evidence to charge Basciano and that Marinakos had been granted immunity in exchange for his testimony. The racial issue would continue through the lengthy appeal process that Campbell launched with the support of the local NAACP.

Judge Bronson also heard several victim impact statements from those who had been injured and from the family members of those who had died.

Nancy Winkler told the judge that the events of June 5, 2013, had changed her forever. "Not a day goes by that I don't miss Anne and mourn her," she said of her daughter. After she left the courthouse that day, she and her husband told reporters, "full justice did not happen in this trial."

Mariya was unable to attend the sentencing hearing because of medical problems, but as one of the victim impact statements, I submitted to the court and read aloud a letter she had written.

In the letter, Mariya wrote, "The doctors tell me I will live to a normal age, but my life will be anything but normal." Then, pointing to the still pending civil litigation, she added, "I do look forward to when all people responsible for what happened . . . will be brought to justice."

Amen.

Key Construction-Related Players in the Litigation

Above: left, Richard Basciano, property owner;
right, Plato Marinakos, architect

Below: left, Griffin Campbell, contractor;
right, Sean Benschop, heavy machinery operator

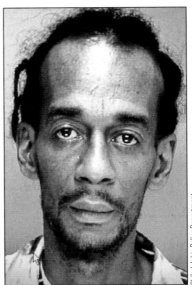

**Key Salvation Army Players
in the Litigation**

*Above: Major Charles Deitrick, General
Secretary for the Eastern Territory*

*Right: Major John Cranford,
Regional Administrator*

The Salvation Army Thrift Store, before contruction began on Market Street

The Demolition Scene

*Above: The Hoagie City building on the day before the collapse;
the unbraced, free-standing wall is at the right*

*Below: The demolition site and the Salvation Army store on the morning
of June 5, 2013, shortly before the disaster*

The corner of 22nd and Market Streets,
right after the collapse, June 5, 2013

February 7, 2013	STRUCTURAL CONDITION OF BUILDING BARELY SOUND
May 9, 2013	"TO PREVENT ANY ACCIDENTS AND DAMAGE TO YOUR PROPERTY . . . WE WOULD REQUIRE ACCESS . . . TIME IS OF THE ESSENCE"
May 10, 2013	"TIME SENSITIVE . . . EVERY MINUTE THAT PASSES INCREASES THE LIABILITY EXPOSURE FOR ALL PARTIES."
May 13, 2013	"URGENT MATTER . . . YOUR RESPONSE IS REQUIRED TO AVOID POTENTIAL DANGER TO SUBJECT PROPERTIES AS WELL AS THE PUBLIC."
May 15, 2013	"MATTER OF URGENCY . . . THE GREATER THE RISKS TO THE PUBLIC AND ALL PROPERTY OWNERS OF UNCONTROLLED COLLAPSE . . ."
May 16, 2013	" . . . CONTINUED DELAYS IN RESPONDING POSE A THREAT TO LIFE, LIMB, AND PUBLIC SAFETY."
May 31, 2013	"TIME IS OF THE ESSENCE . . . NECESSARY TO ACCOMPLISH THE DEMOLITION IN A TIMELY MATTER AND TO MINIMIZE RISK, DANGER, AND EXPENSE."

Summary of the warnings about the danger; an exhibit used at trial,
prepared by Elizabeth Crawford, Esq.

The rescue of Mariya Plekan,
thirteen hours after the building collapse

Mariya Plekan

Above: Mariya Plekan in 2011, with her daughter, Natalia

Right: Mariya on April 21, 2014, at the Hospital of the University of Pennsylvania

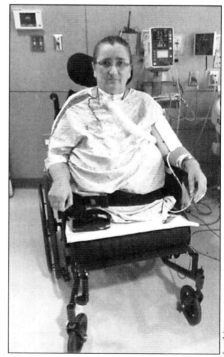

Sam Zolten

Mariya and her family
Left to right: Mariya, Ulyana (daughter-in-law), Natalia (daughter),
Victoria (granddaughter), Ihor (son-in-law), Andrew (son)

Andrew Stern with Mariya in her new home

Elizabeth Crawford

CHAPTER TEN

IT TURNED OUT to be one of the longest trials in the history of Philadelphia Common Pleas Court. In September 2016, when we started picking a jury, no one imagined that it would take so long. In fact, many in the legal community mistakenly anticipated a prompt settlement. But then again, a lot of things that came up during this trial were unexpected.

We knew going in that the defense would consist of lots of finger-pointing. The evidence and deposition testimony supported that. The Salvation Army continued to portray itself as a victim and as an institution blameless for what happened. Marinakos, of course, blamed Campbell and Benschop. Basciano blamed Marinakos and Thomas Simmonds, his project manager.

But all defendants in the courtroom did have one common and potent defense that never changed from day one—that the accident was caused by a dangerous condition created by an incompetent contractor and an excavator operator high on marijuana. And, of course, those two defendants, Campbell and Benschop, had already been found guilty—one by a Philadelphia jury and the other via a guilty plea.

The emails were clearly one of our best pieces of evidence. However, Simmonds's emails warning of the danger were largely dismissed by the defense as posturing and hyperbole. In one of the great twists in the case, Simmonds had conceded that point in his deposition, claiming that his warnings were so much "puffing," part of an effort to convince the Salvation Army (which he referred to in one memo as a "half-baked charity") to allow STB access to the roof.

The irony, which we hoped would not be lost on the jury, was that his warnings turned out to be horribly accurate. The hyperbole became reality.

That point was crucial to the case we wanted to present on behalf of Mariya Plekan. But we were hamstrung at the start when Judge Teresa Sarmina granted a defense motion to prohibit us from introducing damage-related evidence associated with the legal claim of intentional in-fliction of emotional distress. That, the judge ruled, would have to be presented during the damages phase of the trial, depending on whom the jurors found responsible. I wanted the full text of that claim to be part of the liability phase. Specifically, it was my argument that the claim of intentional infliction of emotional distress requires proof of ex-treme and outrageous conditions and evidence of harm suffered by the plaintiff; the two cannot be properly bifurcated or separated.

Of all the plaintiffs, Mariya clearly had the best claim of intentional infliction of emotional distress because she had survived horrific inju-ries and would be able to discuss the emotional impact of that trauma in front of a jury. Further, this was a critically important claim because, as discussed earlier, if we proved intentional misconduct, the Salvation Army would be on the hook for the full verdict regardless of findings of fault relating to other parties. Despite voluminous legal briefs and exten-sive legal arguments, however, we lost our ability to pursue that claim in the liability phase of the case—and that's where we needed that claim the most.

We—Liz Crawford and I—were also troubled by the fact that the other plaintiff attorneys not only did not join in our motion, but rather opposed it along with all of the defense lawyers. Jerome Gamburg com-mented that he could not recall an instance in his fifty years of practice when a group of fellow plaintiffs' lawyers had opposed another plaintiff's claim. The other plaintiffs opposed our claim principally because they contended it would require them to call some of their experts in both the liability and damage phases of the case. Reality kicked in at that point; if indeed we were all supposed to be a "band of brothers," Liz and I were not on the same stage as other members of that ensemble.

It is difficult in a case like this to separate the emotional and the per-sonal from the judicial. Here was our situation throughout the trial: Our client was alive, and it could be reasonably argued that she suffered the most of all the victims; in fact, she was still suffering every minute of every day and would do so for the rest of her life.

Were Mariya's injuries, however severe and crippling, greater than the loss of life? From an economic standpoint in a personal injury case, there was no doubt. No other plaintiff had a claim for future medical expenses projected at close to $50 million.

But our argument also rested on a personal issue. It was not a question any of us wanted to discuss. It just sat there, casting a dark shadow over the multifaceted case we as plaintiff attorneys wanted to present to the jury. On one hand, there was no question that the surviving family members experienced devastating mental suffering from the loss of their loved ones, and that would continue for the rest of their lives. However, Mariya's *physical* pain and suffering, *and* mental anguish and misery, were a never-ending form of torture that she personally endured every day. Furthermore, she would need millions of dollars to pay for the medical attention and everyday care that were now a permanent part of her life. Those were the stakes going in. And once we did the math, it was clear that the only way she would be able to have some small semblance of normalcy in the next decades of her life was for us to win a verdict that provided her with the financial support to cover her needs.

That relief would not come from a judgment against Campbell or Benschop or Marinakos. And it wouldn't come from a judgment against Basciano and STB. The deep pockets in this case belonged to the Salvation Army. And our case had to focus on that institution. Nonetheless, our difficulty with the other plaintiff attorneys was another haunting reminder that Mariya could end up with nothing, a danger that led to countless sleepless nights for her trial lawyers.

During trial, every judicial ruling and every piece of evidence or testimony that deflected attention from the Salvation Army worked against our plan. Going into the trial, we had to be ready not only to present our case and arguments, but also to counteract any move by the defense (or by our fellow plaintiff attorneys) that worked against our focused goal.

As previously mentioned, Robert Mongeluzzi presents himself as a specialist in construction cases. He is recognized nationally as one of the best plaintiff attorneys in those matters. So it was only natural that his primary focus would be on the demolition—specifically, the incompetent manner in which the Hoagie City building was being taken down. One jury had already solidified that claim. The criminal convictions of Benschop and Campbell supported that position completely. Mongeluzzi also had the courtroom status that came with the jury's knowledge that he represented nine plaintiffs in the case, far more than any other lawyer and, in fact, nearly half of those who had filed suit. In addition, early in the trial, the judge mentioned in front of the jurors that Mongeluzzi was an "expert" in construction matters, and this boosted his credibility even more.

Mongeluzzi and many of the other leading plaintiff lawyers represented victims who had died in the rubble and, accordingly, they all had interests that were in substantial alignment. It should be noted that all of the plaintiff lawyers in this case are independent thinkers and highly intelligent advocates; however, in the context of this case and the authority that Mongeluzzi wielded from the outset, the members of that "band," for the most part, followed Mongeluzzi's lead. Roth and Wigrizer did at times attempt to reach a consensus on disputed issues among the plaintiffs, and Roth was also very helpful with the legal issues that were common to all plaintiffs at trial. Regardless, as he articulated in the news media from the very beginning, Mongeluzzi had staked out the faulty demolition as the primary cause of the tragedy; therefore, to attempt to ignore those statements or take a contrary view would have been extremely difficult.

"It was clear they did not have a clue what they were doing," Mongeluzzi said within a week after the accident in June of 2013, according to the news report in the *Philadelphia Inquirer*. "They had a building without steel. It should have been done by hand." That assessment guided him and those who fell in line behind him, particularly the lawyers who represented victims who were not legally permitted to pursue the Salvation Army in our litigation.

But we were not always at odds. When we prevailed on common issues, such as the court's denial of most of the defense motions before the start of trial, there was a wonderful feeling of teamwork and happiness. And there were some really fun moments that we shared outside the office as well. For instance, we would celebrate certain victories during the trial with team outings at a Philadelphia Flyers game. Bob Mongeluzzi's firm had terrific seats directly behind the goal where the Philadelphia Flyers shot two out of three periods. Mongeluzzi's firm graciously offered those seats, which included beverages and food, thereby allowing all of us to take a short break from our suits and ties and enjoy the pleasure of each other's company. Liz would join us in these outings, and I think everyone got a kick out of seeing her there with the rest of us, holding a cheeseburger in one hand and a beer in the other. In these moments, it felt like old times with my friends, and I would almost forget about our disagreements. In fact, I *wanted* to forget about the strained relationships and stressful professional encounters. Unified team efforts, cooperation and camaraderie leave you feeling energized and rejuvenated; but, as the Rolling Stones pointed out, "You can't always get want you want."

Indeed, sometimes the day after these amicable events, when our private strategy sessions placed too much emphasis on the pursuit of the construction-related defendants, we were once again at odds. In the face of significant disagreements, Mongeluzzi would threaten to call for a "democratic" vote. The outcome in that scenario was not surprising in light of the common interests among the attorneys representing the death cases. In addition, the fact that Mongeluzzi had filed the first lawsuit was a basis for agreeing with him because of the leverage he could exert—namely, that he would be legally permitted to present his case first. I found it somewhat ironic that he could be allowed to present first even though the Salvation Army was not included in his initial suit. Occasionally, one of the plaintiff lawyers would speak up in opposition, but it was often short-lived. On one occasion, a lawyer speaking in opposition was told to "stand down." I fully recognize that litigation is not for the faint of heart, and I truly admire aggressive and zealous advocacy from my adversaries, but as a former political science major at the Pennsylvania State University, it reminded of Alexis de Tocqueville's phrase *tyranny of the majority.*

When I voiced my concerns about the lack of sufficient emphasis on the Salvation Army, I was sometimes criticized for being stubborn and not acting like a "team player." Mongeluzzi would also frequently remind me, in the presence of the other plaintiff lawyers, of his vast conquests in other construction-related cases such as the Philadelphia Pier 34 and Duck Boat litigations, as well as his experience in a garage collapse case at the Tropicana Casino in Atlantic City. While I had experience in other construction-related matters, it admittedly paled in comparison to Mongeluzzi's, and so this was used as additional leverage to persuade the plaintiff team that he knew best. Much as I wanted to be a team player, I refused to equivocate on my theme that this case involved much more than demolition. I was raised by my father to be thick-skinned, and I didn't let the criticism get to me, but because Mongeluzzi was a friend it definitely bothered me at times. Although I did not want to lose a friendship in this process, I viewed my representation of Mariya as much more than merely my job.

I quickly figured out that if Liz and I were going to succeed at principally focusing blame on the Salvation Army, we would have to persuade the jury with the *quality* of the evidence, not the *quantity*. In our view, this had been one of the problems during the discovery process, when substantial amounts of time and money were concentrated on parties who had little or no money, and who were not at the root of the problem that led to the catastrophic building collapse.

For example, during the discovery phase of the case, seven days were spent taking depositions from Basciano and his related companies, when they had already placed their relatively limited amount of settlement money in escrow at the *beginning* of the case. Six days were spent taking the deposition of Marinakos, the architect who had no money. Four days were spent taking the deposition of Campbell, the contractor who was sitting in jail with no money. Three days were spent taking the deposition of Benschop, the excavator who also was a pawn in this process and was sitting in jail with no money.

After Mongeluzzi had finished his lead questioning of Griffin Campbell at his deposition, I practically pleaded with him to give Campbell an opportunity to discuss a crucial fact: that he knew nothing about the Salvation Army's decision to deny access to the Thrift Store property. Mongeluzzi refused, and none of the other plaintiff lawyers put any pressure on him to do so. So I myself asked Campbell those questions, and his answers were commanding and directly on point:

STERN: I will represent to you that Mr. Nudel sent an internal email to representatives associated with the Salvation Army on May 21st where the email said that they were not going to give access, and he testified that those were "his words." I'm going to represent that he said that at a deposition. I'm going to represent to you that he also testified that he did not let anybody know on the part of STB or the demolition people that that was his decision, and he had his reasons, but I'm going to represent to you that he admits he didn't tell people like yourself.

CAMPBELL: So why am I going to jail for fifteen or thirty years . . .

STERN: And what I want to ask you about, though, is in light of that, as of May 21st, or even May 22nd, or even May 23rd, if it had been brought to your attention that the Salvation Army had basically determined they were not going to give access . . .

CAMPBELL: In the job . . .
STERN: In terms of your approach.
CAMPBELL: The job would have had to stop.

Campbell's testimony was that everything would have stopped if he had been told that the Salvation Army would not allow access to the roof!

In any event, there were more than forty additional depositions involving construction-related individuals. While it is true that the total length of the depositions was not solely due to questions by plaintiffs' counsel, a substantial amount of time was spent on those inquiries. Yes, the lawyers were well-prepared, but the protracted nature of these depositions would have been necessary *only if* the owner, architect and construction-related defendants had the ability to satisfy a large monetary judgment and had not already put up their money. I recognized that we had to meet our burden of proof in offering evidence against these defendants, but the amount of time spent on their depositions was overkill, and it was much less challenging to prove liability against these parties as compared to the Salvation Army. Not only was I frustrated; I was concerned that this course of action could divert attention from the one party that had plenty of money and good potential liability.

The issue of access to the Salvation Army roof led to another disagreement among the plaintiff attorneys. Steve Estrin, a construction expert hired by Mongeluzzi, was viewed as one of our key witnesses because of his plan to discuss how the building was dangerous in mid-May, at the time the warning emails were being sent. In my view, the emails were critical to proving that the Salvation Army had knowledge of a potential danger but ignored the warnings, and that the Army's continued refusal to provide roof access to the contractor significantly contributed to the ultimate collapse. However, as it turned out, Estrin and/or Bob Mongeluzzi determined that Estrin's testimony would directly criticize only the architect, contractor and excavator. Estrin did not offer any criticism of the Salvation Army, nor did he discuss the need for roof access. I practically begged Mongeluzzi to have "our" expert, who charged a substantial amount of money, consider the access theory in order to better tie in the emails and the Salvation Army. Both Mongeluzzi and his partner, Jeff Goodman, vehemently resisted, telling me that the "access theory" was not a viable theory and the Salvation Army had no legal duty to provide access. They also argued that the failure to grant access did not contribute to the collapse. With Liz's effective assistance, we made legal arguments actually citing case law. But they still did not want to listen. We were literally told to stop wasting everyone's time with the "access theory."

I should add that while Mongeluzzi was my good friend at the outset of the case, Goodman was one of Liz's friends. He had been in her social circle during law school and thereafter. Initially, I think it was difficult for Liz, as a younger lawyer, to speak up and take a strong position that was contrary not only to a well-respected and experienced construction lawyer (Mongeluzzi), but also to her friend and someone she respected, Goodman. As time progressed, Liz grew much less hesitant to speak up and became a persuasive voice of reason in the midst of disagreements, even those involving her friends.

As it turned out, I had no alternative but to hire another demolition/construction expert who would address the access theory. The expert was Bill Moore. He was highly qualified in construction and demolition. His field experience involved planning and oversight on more than 300 demolition projects, including: (1) the largest steel mill ever demolished—USS Gary Works merchant mills (Gary, Indiana); (2) the largest mine—BHP Copper (San Manuel, Arizona); (3) the largest brownfield site—Bethlehem Steel (Bethlehem, Pennsylvania); (4) the largest timber frame building—Sears Catalogue Warehouse (Chicago, Illinois); and (5) the longest implosion—Veterans Stadium (Philadelphia, Pennsylvania). Because of his effective assistance, we were able to defeat the Salvation Army's attempts to preclude plaintiffs from introducing evidence that the Salvation Army owed any duty of access to the neighboring property. If Jack Snyder had convinced the judge that access was irrelevant to the case, this would have paved the way for the Salvation Army to preclude a lot of powerful evidence.

Ultimately, we did not call Bill Moore to the witness stand at trial. Nor did we call certain other experts, in part because of the way our evidence had unfolded and in part because of anticipated objections that the testimony would, in large measure, be cumulative. ("Cumulative" testimony—similar or identical testimony offered by more than one witness—is often limited by a court.) Nonetheless, the experts were effective in buttressing the legal theories in our case, as well as defeating various pretrial motions filed by the Salvation Army. Moreover, because the defense knew that we had the ability to call an expert to establish the connection with access theory, we were better able to explore the theory with other witnesses.

With all this jockeying among attorneys in the background, the trial testimony finally began. The first witness Mongeluzzi called in the case was Steve Estrin, the construction/demolition expert. Estrin was on the stand for four days. His testimony laid liability at the feet of Campbell, Benschop, Marinakos, Basciano and STB. At no time during those four days did Estrin ever say or imply that the Salvation Army was responsible, in whole or in part, for the catastrophic collapse and resulting injuries and deaths.

Though Steve Estrin is a gifted trial expert, it was difficult for me to sit there and listen at times, especially when I noticed that the lawyers for the Salvation Army appeared to be nodding in agreement. After all, the Salvation Army was blaming the same individuals. Jack Snyder, lead trial counsel for the Salvation Army, had *no* questions on cross for Estrin. But then again, why would he? Snyder liked what he was hearing.

In my opening statement, I started by telling the jury that they would get to learn *"a lot"* about the Salvation Army. The sarcasm in my voice telegraphed that there was much more to this organization than one might think, and I could see a twinkle in the eyes of a few jurors in response. I told the jury that the Salvation Army had a responsibility to "investigate, communicate and vacate," a phrase coined by Harry Roth in response to the vast amount of incriminating evidence we had developed against this charitable entity during discovery. We were in court, I said, because the charity had done none of those things, and I provided specific examples of our evidence to support my theories.

The Salvation Army, I argued, had ignored the warnings. They hired a wallpaper and paint company official to assess structural damage. They deliberately and coldly denied access to the roof. And now they wanted to claim that those warnings were the exaggerated rantings of an STB official who was trying to take advantage of them. The charity was more concerned about property damage than safety, I said. Their officials talked about "neighborly goals" in discussions with STB, but the only real goal was protecting an investment. Throughout my opening, I offered no criticisms of anyone but the Salvation Army.

Two of the first witnesses called in the case set the stage for the jury's understanding of the tragedy. Felicia Hill, a Thrift Store employee who had managed to get out, testified about working conditions in the store and how employees "would talk about like how the building was shaking. Like every day the shaking. . . . And we would like . . . kind of joke about it."

I then called John O'Neill, by then a Battalion Chief, and had him explain the rescue operation, the tick-tock of the recovery of the bodies and the miraculous discovery of Mariya in the rubble late on the night of June 5, 2013. Chief O'Neill was clearly one of the heroes of this tragic story. O'Neill's testimony painted a picture of the enormity of the disaster—and the magnitude of the risk that was involved before the collapse occurred.

I also wanted the jury to hear from people like Margarita Agosto, the Thrift Store manager, who during her deposition had cut to the very heart of the case when she said, "That's not right what happened. People lost their life, a lady's legs, you know? I get to see my family. You know what I mean? The people that died, Kimberly, she don't get to go back to her life. That's gone. Borbor is gone. That poor lady has to live with no legs. That's not cool.

"Regardless of whose fault it was, it should never have happened. Never. It should have been taken care of way before. Way before."

I would call Margarita later in the trial, and she would repeat many of the things she had told us during her deposition. During my opening, I described Agosto's anticipated testimony as believable But we—myself and her attorney Jerome Gamburg—would have to counter attempts by other attorneys who wanted to blame her, in part, for failing to close the store. In fact, a retail expert called by another plaintiff lawyer suggested as much. Again, this deflected from our case. If a jury believed that Margarita Agosto could have closed the Thrift Store, then it might decide that the Salvation Army upper management was not responsible, or had limited responsibility and had not engaged in intentional misconduct. I always believed Agosto was credible and was convinced a jury would too—this was another calculated risk I decided to take, and it worked.

It was also important, I believed, for the jurors to hear from Benschop and Campbell. I preferred live testimony, but the jury heard from them through the video depositions both men had given. Their comments about the demolition project were consistent with what each had said during the criminal trial. But from our perspective that was a secondary issue.

The jury needed to see both men, at least by video, and hear them, and understand the roles both played in this tragedy. They painted themselves as scapegoats. I was inclined to agree. Yes, there was a good argument that their actions were incompetent, but did that rise to a level of criminal intent? Besides, our contention was that the owner (Basciano) and his representatives knew that you get what you pay for, and purposely chose to hire these inexperienced demo guys to save money.

During his deposition, Benschop, who couldn't read or write and who at times struggled with his vocabulary, asked a simple question. "Why you all didn't close the building down as Griffin Campbell could get access?" he asked. "The Salvation Army close down for two days the building would have been taken down and then we . . . we wasn't going to be here. I wasn't going to be in jail. Griffin Campbell wasn't going to be in jail. . . . You sitting up here blaming me. Everybody blaming each other and nobody taking responsibility. . . . You could replace the building, but you can't replace the life of the people that died. . . . For what?"

It was very interesting to me and Liz that when I got to question Campbell and Benschop about issues relating to access to the Salvation Army Thrift Store, they certainly didn't think it was irrelevant and a waste of time.

I had asked Campbell if anyone had ever told him about the warnings or if anyone had ever offered to give him access to the roof. His answer painted a picture of the principal players in the drama.

"The only one I talked with was Plato [Marinakos]," he said. "And we all know what he did. He ran. We all know what Basciano did. He ran. And do you want to hear the truth? The Salvation Army ran. They ran. They put this burden on my shoulder, like I was the guy calling the shots. I didn't call any shots. . . .

"The minute the wall fell, what did they do immediately? Oh, let's give this land now to the victims' family. Let's give land to the victims' family. You could have avoided all that. All you had to do was give me access."

That was the essence of our case. And, yes, the only defendant who could have granted access was the Salvation Army.

I intended to use the testimony of both Margarita Agosto and Edward Strudwick to give the jury an inside, humanistic look at what was going on in the months leading up to the collapse. I also thought they would help me portray a different face of the "benevolent" Salvation Army. But before that, I called a retail safety expert, Robert Bartlett, early in the trial to give the jury what I hoped it would see as an objective assessment of the situation.

Born and educated in London, Bartlett, the head of California-based Bartlett Joseph Associates, was a forty-year veteran of the retail consulting business. His clients have included The Gap, Banana Republic, Costco and the Burlington Coat Factory, among others. He had been involved in almost all aspects of a retail store operation, from construction design to day-to-day management practices. And while Jack Snyder, the attorney for the Salvation Army, challenged both his credentials and his testimony, I thought his time on the witness stand solidified the foundation for our case. Bottom line, Bartlett came off as a credible witness, and I could tell the jury liked him.

With his British accent and his no-nonsense, cut-to-the-chase responses, he focused on what any retail store operator should have done. That was the point we needed the jury to understand. The Salvation Army Thrift Store was a retail business just like Macy's or The Gap or Target or the Burlington Coat Factory. When those businesses open their doors, they are telling their customers it is safe to come and shop. It's not something that a customer often thinks about, but it is a tacit understanding, part of an unspoken business contract between a store and its shoppers.

Bartlett, who at my request had reviewed all the memos and emails between STB and the Salvation Army, offered a detailed picture of responsibility. He told the jury that, based on his readings of those documents, it was clear the Salvation Army had continually ignored the warnings and deliberately had failed to communicate. He added that in the retail business safety was "an overarching priority."

"The store should have been closed on or before June 4," he said, adding the obvious: if it had been closed, the disaster would not have happened.

He talked about safety standards and what is expected in the retail business, and he pointed out that the Salvation Army, with 280 thrift stores in the region that included Philadelphia, would be considered a major retailer. Regardless of the size and scope of its business, he added, the charity had the same obligations to its customers when it opened its doors.

"Since they are a significant retailer operating all these stores with a trusted brand that's been around forever and that people trust to go shopping in, they absolutely have the same non-delegable obligation to keep both the customers and the employees working in that store safe," he said.

"You have a fundamental obligation to provide safety for both customers and employees. That's not negotiable."

And based on industry standards and his assessment of the situation, he said, "The store should have been closed, no doubt." Indeed, Bartlett effectively used the Salvation Army's own standards, which require its employees to report and address potential safety hazards, to buttress his opinions.

At another point he said, "if an appropriate person had visited the site on or before June 4, they would have immediately contacted the Salvation Army and got the store closed down until the situation could be resolved."

But at no time did the Salvation Army send anyone with authority to take a look at what was going on next door.

I took Bartlett through what we, as plaintiff attorneys, had listed as seven warnings that went out prior to the collapse, beginning with Marinakos's assessment of the structural disrepair of the Thrift Store building in February 2013 and ending with Simmonds's warnings of death and destruction written a few months later.

"It should have been prevented," Bartlett said of the collapse. "[B]y the time they had the seventh warning, the risk was total."

He continually hammered away at the Salvation Army's indifference and seeming lack of concern, mentioning again that its first response to Marinakos's memo was to send a paint and wallpaper company official rather than a structural engineer.

During his time on the witness stand, I played him part of Major Cranford's video deposition, including Cranford's comment that there was no need to alert store employees to any potential danger because it wasn't their business.

Bartlett's response zeroed in on another point we wanted to make. The employees, he said, "had the right to be safe themselves and they had an obligation to keep the customers safe." Without that information, he said, "they were blind-sided by the disaster."

In what amounted to a summary of his testimony, he told the jury, "Any retail company that I've ever been associated with would have taken management action given the potential hazard and warnings that were coming in."

Asked about management failure on the part of the Salvation Army, he replied, "Management failure is why I'm sitting in this chair today."

Snyder tried to undermine Bartlett's responses and continually challenged his description of industry standards, asking repeatedly where such standards were written. Bartlett wasn't bullied, nor did he back away.

At one point, in response to a question from Snyder, who continually tried to downplay what we had described as the "warnings," Bartlett drove home another point in support of our case.

"So what was in play, as far as the Salvation Army senior management was concerned, was about safety," he said. "And in all these discussions and all these emails, there is scant discussion of the safety of the customers and the people in the store and what steps that the Salvation Army management team were going to do to make sure that they were kept safe.

"It was a fundamental responsibility they had and they seemed not to have been preoccupied with it. In fact, they withheld information from the one person on the ground, Miss Agosto, who turned up for work on June 5. She was left in the dark."

With that comment, Bartlett had offered unequivocal support for Agosto's conduct. He went on to call the Salvation Army's conduct "reckless." Not surprisingly, there was an immediate loud objection from Snyder, which led to a long sidebar conference outside the hearing of the jury. During the sidebar, I contended that the expert testimony was relevant to the punitive conduct we were permitted to argue in the first phase of the trial and that Bartlett was competent to offer that opinion Judge Sarmina overruled the objection. Bartlett also effectively discussed the evidence that I had uncovered about other instances when the Salvation Army had temporarily closed a thrift store due to concerns about a potential safety hazard.

A few days later, I called Edward Strudwick to the stand. And even later in the trial I would question Margarita Agosto. They both repeated for the jury what they had already told us during their depositions.

Strudwick described what we saw as the callous indifference of Major Cranford even in the face of questions his own wife raised about the safety of the demolition work.

Joe Slobodzian, the court reporter for the *Philadelphia Inquirer*, captured the essence of Strudwick's testimony when he wrote that a witness had focused on "petty bickering and an autocratic administrator."

A recovering alcoholic who readily admitted he had benefited from and was grateful for the charity's rehabilitation program, Strudwick had no axe to grind. Furthermore, Strudwick was honest about everything, including a flaw relating to alcoholism that he had learned to control. This, I believe, made his testimony even more credible as he told the jury of the May 22, 2013, staff meeting that occurred only two weeks before the collapse. In that meeting, Strudwick, who was working as a truck dispatcher for the Salvation Army, recalled that Cranford showed no intention of letting anyone from STB on the roof of the Thrift Store and gruffly dismissed the concerns his wife raised with his one-hurdle-at-a-time comment. Cranford, Strudwick said, seemed to be "concerned with damage to the roof, damage to the building, not the people."

Strudwick also said that Cranford "had a closed-door policy, not an open-door policy. . . . It was his way or no way." In sum, Strudwick got the jurors to start to believe that certain members of the Salvation Army were capable of misconduct.

Later, Agosto gave the jury a picture of what it was like in the store in the weeks leading up to and on the day of the disaster. And how, through it all, she had been, in the words of Robert Bartlett, "blindsided" and "left in the dark."

At that point, I felt I was delivering some of what I had promised in my opening when I told the jurors that they would "get to learn *a lot* about this organization called the Salvation Army."

CHAPTER ELEVEN

THE STORY OF ANY major trial, civil or criminal, is built around the evidence and the testimony from the witness stand. In addition, pretrial depositions and motions help set the stage and offer dramatic twists and turns even before a jury is selected. The atmosphere in the courtroom and the ebb and flow of spectators provide other elements. Most important, a prudent trial lawyer should always expect the unexpected.

We were meeting every day in an ornate and large sixth-floor courtroom (Room 653) in the iconic Philadelphia City Hall building at the intersection of Broad and Market Streets, in the heart of the metropolis William Penn had mapped out more than three centuries ago.

And I was more than happy to be there.

There had been talk, because of all the pretrial publicity, of changing venue. The defense favored moving the trial away from the city—that is, except the Salvation Army, which appeared comfortable allowing a Philadelphia jury to assess the evidence. We adamantly opposed any change of venue. The last thing we wanted was a jury selected from somewhere in the middle of Pennsylvania. Instead, we wanted Philadelphians, i.e., open-minded jurors who would have a better understanding of the backstory and the community where this tragedy occurred.

In the previous chapter I described how the case opened. Now I want to back up a bit to talk about how the jurors were chosen.

It took about a week in September 2016 to select a panel, which included twelve jurors and six alternates. Judge Sarmina, a dedicated, hard-working and "no bullshit" jurist, put a tight lid on the process. Judge Sarmina worked countless hours on this case and was determined to ensure everyone would get a fair trial. All the lawyers in the case were placed under a gag order that prohibited us from discussing or commenting on the case—and may God have mercy on your soul if you breached Her Honor's order! Judge Sarmina commands and receives a tremendous level of respect from the trial bar. At a minimum, you'd better be prepared and you'd better be on time.

All the jurors were chosen anonymously. Picking a jury is an inexact science, really more of an art form. Some attorneys put stock in having a consultant at the table during the process to assess each potential juror. I think that's overrated. You have to go with your gut, your instinct. I like jurors who display common sense with no hidden agenda. I also like jurors who show intelligence and have the potential to sift through the rhetoric and drill down to the basics. Learning about someone's life experiences is important, but how they have reacted to those experiences and their outlook on life are of paramount importance.

The selection process includes questioning each potential juror individually. This is called *voir dire*. The purpose is to allow the attorneys to get a sense of the individual. At a minimum, trial counsel should be given a brief opportunity to meet individually with the jurors in a separate room outside the presence of other jurors during the selection process—that's where you can draw your most accurate impressions.

Jurors whose answers indicate they could not or would not be fair and impartial are dismissed "for cause." Each side in the case also has a fixed number of challenges that can be used arbitrarily to dismiss a potential juror for any reason, provided the challenge does not involve unlawful discrimination.

Going into the process, each defendant entity (the STB defendants; the Salvation Army defendants; the Marinakos defendants; and the Griffin Campbell defendants) had four challenges, and the plaintiffs collectively had four challenges. This arrangement was presumably devised in part by Judge Sarmina to address certain defendants' arguments that they could not get a fair trial in Philadelphia County. We, the plaintiffs, used most of our challenges over the week-long process. I was particularly pleased when a handful of potential jurors who appeared suspiciously motivated to offer the "right" answers were nixed. I worry that anyone who is too anxious to be picked, and who seems to offer rehearsed answers to questions, may already have preconceived notions or motivations about the case.

The jury selection process and serving as a juror are pivotal aspects of our judicial system. The jurors chosen all said they would be able to deliver a fair and impartial verdict. Most said they had heard about the case. It would be hard to believe anyone living in the Philadelphia area hadn't. But, for the most part, they said their knowledge was limited. Most on the panel knew several people had been killed, but surprisingly only a few jurors had heard about the grievous injuries Mariya had sustained. The jurors who were ultimately selected all expressed an unwavering and credible ability to be fair, and this put to rest any concerns about the need for a change of venue. The jury that was ultimately selected was superb.

Each and every day, Judge Sarmina told the jurors not to read, look at or listen to any media accounts of the trial and not to discuss the case in any way with anyone. Evidence and testimony should be their focus, and any judicial questions would be explained by the judge during the trial. At the beginning of the trial, Her Honor also told the jurors that if there was a breach of the court's order, the ramifications could be draconian, including the possibility of declaring a mistrial, which could also result in the imposition of harsh monetary sanctions and other severe penalties against the offending juror. Without question, I believe that all of the jurors strictly followed the court's terse instructions.

Nancy Winkler, whose daughter, Anne Bryan, was one of the victims, was in court almost every day, taking notes and studying witnesses. Her presence was a reminder of the terrible loss she and other victims' family members had suffered. Even without taking the stand, her presence bore witness and could not have been missed by the jury. Other victims and family members, including Mariya, were in court as well. Even though she wanted to come every day, Mariya, for health reasons, was there only a few times. When she was present, she definitely attracted attention.

The Salvation Army also had a visible presence. Witnesses who testified, like Colonel Raines and Majors Deitrick and Cranford, showed up in uniform. So did a half dozen other Salvation Army regulars. They came to court each day dressed in identical white shirts, red ties, dark (navy blue or black) slacks and matching blazers with red epaulets and red patches with the large letter S on each lapel. They would sit front and center in the spectator section of the courtroom, directly behind the defense tables. They were like extras on a movie set, men and women of different ages and races. The personnel would change, but a uniformed contingent appeared in court each day of the proceedings. Their presence was designed, I believe, to send a message to the jury: "You know us. We're the charity that has been doing good works for more than a century." Within that contingent there was always a female representative.

When I called Ed Strudwick to the stand—a man who had worked for the Salvation Army during the time period in question—I pointed to the Salvation Army group that was sitting in the courtroom that day and asked if he knew any of them. He said he did not. I think the jury got the point.

The trial began in September and stretched through the holiday season and into 2017. This created another issue. During the Christmas season, the Salvation Army always stations workers at the four entrances to the City Hall complex. These are large, arched, European-style outdoor halls that lead to a mini piazza around which City Hall is built. Jurors coming to court each day would have to pass a uniformed Salvation Army worker ringing a bell and asking passersby to drop donations into the large Salvation Army kettle. More than the uniformed presence in the courtroom, this was the symbol of the Salvation Army.

We had successfully argued in a pretrial motion that Salvation Army witnesses would not be identified as ministers, even though most of them were ordained. The judge accepted our argument that identifying a witness as a minister of a church would unfairly enhance credibility and thus interfere with an objective assessment of a given witness. What we had no control over was a juror's perception of the Salvation Army bell and kettle that he or she would pass each day during the holiday season. The judge addressed the issue briefly without belaboring the point. Jurors were told that they were to focus only on the testimony and evidence and not any extraneous issues. But I have to admit that my heart dropped slightly when one of the jurors, in response to the judge's comments, asked if it would still be all right to make a donation—to drop some cash into the kettle—before coming to court. Yikes!

All of that was part of the backstory of the trial. Like the testimony and evidence, it could have made an impact on the jury. We were constantly on watch for anything that might undermine our issues and the narrative we wanted the jury to follow.

Joe Slobodzian, the *Inquirer*'s standout court reporter, reported what was happening at trial and hardly missed a day of court, even though the case dragged on for months. But the articles relating to parties other than the Salvation Army were sometimes so pronounced that we had people—who had not been in the courtroom—asking us if the Salvation Army was really in the case. In all fairness, Slobodzian was accurately reporting what was occurring in court. A lot of the evidence was being aimed at other parties, not directly at the Salvation Army.

The press coverage was disconcerting and at times disheartening. Intellectually, we knew the only thing that mattered was what the jury saw and heard. And we recognized that many of the non–Salvation Army witnesses had a certain level of importance. But from our viewpoint, they were not the key witnesses.

As a result, we had a constant concern that the amount of time devoted to these other witnesses, and the melodrama generated around them, would detract from our ultimate goal.

From our perspective, three witnesses were key—Richard Basciano, Major John Cranford and Major Charles Deitrick. Initially it was believed that Tom Simmonds, who had authored what everyone at the defense table was now calling the "hyperbole" email warnings, would also be significant. But the hyperbole defense theory proved futile because of evidence and testimony about the potential safety hazards the demolition had caused—and, more important, because the warnings had proved true.

Basciano was on the witness stand for parts of three days. Because of his age—he was ninety-one—and health issues, the judge had limited his daily testimony to three hours. At times he presented himself as a serious, hands-on businessman who had a development plan that would have been great for the city. But at other points he appeared to use the shields of old age and failing health in response to questions he could not or did not want to answer.

He described himself as a self-made man, a World War II veteran who came home and used the G.I. Bill to learn a trade. He started as a bricklayer in his native Baltimore and eventually got into the real estate business and moved to New York. With his white hair stylishly coiffed, and impeccably dressed in a suit, shirt and tie, Basciano made a good appearance.

But it didn't last.

He was called as a witness by Steven Wigrizer, who did a great job in challenging Basciano's credibility in a balanced fashion. Mongeluzzi also got to question Basciano and seemed to take pride in the fact that he got the developer to cry, to break down on the stand. But from where we stood, it was Wigrizer who had scored the most damaging blows. Regardless, I viewed this approach as counterproductive because Basciano and his various related corporations clearly did not have the financial ability to satisfy the verdict potential in this litigation. As Basciano's counsel would privately remind the plaintiffs' lawyers with a smile, if anyone other than the Salvation Army is found to be substantially liable, the plaintiffs lose! Unfortunately, from a financial perspective, he was right. Every lawyer in the courtroom knew that. The Salvation Army was the only defendant capable of paying a substantial judgment.

One of the points of contention, indeed one of the unanswered questions as the case moved forward, was what, if anything, Basciano had said and done when the wall came down. Griffin Campbell had testified that he was talking to Basciano and Basciano's wife at the time of the collapse. Campbell said that he had stood with his back to the wall but that the couple was looking directly at it. Campbell even described the shocked look he saw on Lois Basciano's face as the wall crashed into the Thrift Store.

Campbell said he turned and went to help.

Basciano, he said, ran away.

But on the witness stand, Basciano described that as a gross distortion of the facts and a "damn lie."

His story, told both during his deposition and when Wigrizer questioned him in front of the jury, was that he wasn't there when the wall came down. He and his wife arrived that morning, he said, to check on the progress of the demolition work. They had an apartment at the posh Symphony House, a condo complex on Broad Street about ten blocks from the project. They had taken a cab and then walked. Basciano said he didn't really look up at the work as he passed the Thrift Store because he was walking with a cane and had to look down. He had recently had a knee replacement.

"I'm incapacitated," he said.

What's more, he said, after he arrived "I had to go to the bathroom." So, he said, he walked to a parking garage that he owned a few doors away on Market Street. That, he said, was where he was when the wall collapsed. He never saw it go down, although he conceded that when he walked out of the garage, he saw the devastation.

The wall collapsed about 10:41 that morning. Wigrizer questioned Basciano about phone calls that were made from his cell phone and from his wife's cell phone a few minutes later. At 10:47 a.m. his phone showed a two-minute call to the parking garage, and her phone showed a three-minute call to the same number.

When Wigrizer asked about this, Basciano said, "I can't answer that. I don't know if it's fact or fiction." Basciano claimed he had left his cell phone with his wife when he went to the garage to use the bathroom. Why, then, were both cell phones calling the same garage number in the immediate aftermath of the collapse?

Phone records also showed that around 10:49 that morning, Basciano's cell phone listed a call to his office in New York. At the same time, his wife's phone showed a call to a close friend of hers in Morristown, New Jersey. The question Wigrizer asked, but Basciano couldn't answer, was why his wife would be using two phones to simultaneously make two calls to two different numbers. Of course, Wigrizer didn't need an answer to drive home the point.

Basciano said he and his wife walked to a nearby firehouse after the collapse and then took a cab to another section of the city, where he had an appointment with an ophthalmologist.

Richard Basciano was having a routine eye examination as rescuers tried to dig the bodies out of the rubble of the Thrift Store.

More important, Basciano's testimony also included his account of how he had tried to trade properties with the Salvation Army and how they had turned down his "generous" offer. He also insisted that, had he known about the potential dangers, he would have shut the job down. But he said neither Marinakos nor Simmonds, despite the emails and memos that were going back and forth from February to June, had mentioned anything about it to him.

Much of this may have been hard to believe, but once again I was concerned that the discrepancies in the accounts could cause jurors to lose focus on that benevolent organization in the best position to protect the people in the store, i.e., the Salvation Army.

Basciano's confrontation with Mongeluzzi came during his second day on the stand. Basciano had denied any responsibility for what had happened when he was questioned by Steve Wigrizer, often mumbling "I don't remember." He also dramatically told Wigrizer that he was distraught over what had happened, adding, "I'm living in hell." I would have been fine with letting his testimony end on that note.

However, when Wigrizer finished, Mongeluzzi jumped on that response, asking Basciano if he thought the "victims' families are going through hell."

At that point, the developer appeared to lose it on the stand.

"That is exactly why I'm going through hell," he nearly shouted. "When people died, I'm broken-hearted about it. I'm broken-hearted about it."

He then began to sob and told the judge, "I can't go on, Your Honor. I can't go on."

He was dismissed for the day. He made one more brief, uneventful trip to the witness stand when the trial resumed, but from our perspective the jury had seen more than enough to draw its own conclusions about Richard Basciano and his role in what had happened on June 5, 2013. I didn't have any questions for Basciano—I had wanted him off the stand days before. I figured that, at a minimum, jurors must have serious questions about his credibility, and that was good enough for me.

The people in the courtroom who saw Basciano testify had mixed reviews. Some felt sorrow for him and others did not. Of interest, my wife, Gwen, had brought her trial advocacy class to court that day. When court was over, the majority of her students commented that Basciano came across as a feeble old man who had been "beat up" on the stand; surprisingly, they felt bad for him.

We had also hoped to raise credibility questions with three key Salvation Army officials, Lieutenant Colonel Timothy Raines and Majors Charles Deitrick and John Cranford. Raines had testified earlier in the trial. Deitrick and Cranford came after Basciano.

Raines had echoed what would be the common party-line defense when he said, "The life and death situation came about because of the excavator operator. It had nothing to do with a safe demolition. . . . I don't think anybody could have, any normal person could have predicted somebody was going to knock over their building onto ours."

Like other Salvation Army witnesses who followed him, Raines said he believed demolition was not going on and that it would not commence until the question of access to the roof had been resolved. This, of course, was at odds with the various memos and emails, none of which suggested that demolition would be halted until the roof access issue was settled. But the Army adhered to this position throughout the trial.

Raines also said that he and other officials "believed we were dealing with someone I believed to be a credible person—the developer."

Steve Wigrizer, who was handling that portion of the questioning, then pulled out a copy of the internal email Raines had sent back in November 2012, when the Salvation Army was engaged in protracted and difficult negotiations with Basciano and STB over the potential swap of Market Street properties. Raines had written that "these people are not serious and have no credibility. . . . They wouldn't know the truth if it slapped them in the face."

Now Raines was trying to tell the jury that when it came to safety questions and the dangers surrounding the demolition, he was content to depend on the credibility of those same people. Thanks to what Wigrizer had effectively brought out, the contradiction was clear.

Credibility is the most important issue that jurors, as fact finders, have to assess. That's why it was important for the jury not only to hear Raines, but also to see the email in which, through his own words, he contradicted his testimony.

Simply put, if a witness's credibility is questioned, so too is his testimony.

That was a key issue for us when Raines took the stand, and Wigrizer did a really nice job of challenging him in a cool, collected and convincing way.

In our estimation, the question of credibility was even more important when I called Deitrick to testify. As plaintiffs we called a number of adverse witnesses in our case which, under the rules of evidence, permitted us to cross-examine them by asking leading questions. Deitrick clearly was the face the Salvation Army wanted to present to the jury. He had a calming presence. He was solid and dependable. And through his demeanor, he appeared concerned, thoughtful and level-headed. Indeed, he often appeared to be on the verge of genuine tears when he discussed the tragedy. In that regard, he was in complete contrast to Cranford, who appeared more hot-headed and self-centered and showed practically no remorse for what had happened.

Most of the Salvation Army witnesses, not surprisingly, suggested that Deitrick had the greatest involvement in the Thrift Store issues, particularly in the discussions about access and the email warnings. That was another reason why his testimony would prove to be pivotal.

But not everyone was interested in taking him on.

On the day I called him to the stand, I was told by another plaintiff attorney that he did not plan to ask Deitrick any questions. That reflected the way many on our side of the courtroom felt about the major. The reason was clear. We all understood that Deitrick would be the most challenging Salvation Army witness. Some lawyers were concerned that intensive questioning might be perceived as overly aggressive and generate sympathy for him, and ultimately for the charity. It was a fine line, but one I felt I had to walk because I would lead off with his cross-examination.

During our trial preparation we had focused on ways to challenge his credibility. We needed to get the jurors to question whether Deitrick was actually sincere. We wanted them to look beyond the kind words and platitudes and the avuncular demeanor to question whether there was more to the man than met the eye.

In my questioning of the major, I focused on the Salvation Army's own policies and procedures regarding safety and on his avowed lifetime of providing service to people. Deitrick served under Raines as General Secretary of the Salvation Army's Eastern Territory and, in that capacity, was Cranford's superior. From the witness stand he agreed with me when, in response to one of my first questions, he said, "Safety is a top priority."

But he stuck to the position that neither he nor anyone else in command believed there was any danger at the Thrift Store. This was part of the canned "hyperbole" defense, the argument that all the warnings were part of an STB strategy to get access to the roof and perhaps to jump-start new negotiations for a property swap.

"We didn't know of any risks that needed to be shared [with the employees of the store] during any of this time frame," he said at one point. At another he said, "If we knew that there was a danger, we would be responsible to communicate that with them. We did not know."

That flew in the face of the email warnings, which showed evidence of a potential safety hazard. I hoped the jury was following that logic. Liz had created a very helpful exhibit that, in plain and easy-to-follow language, mapped out the numerous warnings given to the Salvation Army relating to safety.

Deitrick was the *only* Salvation Army witness who said that access to the roof had been conditionally granted to STB, a position contrary not only to the facts in the case, but also to the testimony of other Salvation

Army witnesses. That contradiction, we hoped, would further undermine his credibility.

I also tried to use Deitrick's testimony to highlight a key point in our trial strategy. We wanted the jury to focus not on what the Salvation Army officials said, but rather on what they did, or failed to do.

With that in mind, I sprinkled my questions with screen displays of inspirational quotes that Deitrick was fond of: philosophical quotes from Vince Lombardi and other recognized leaders of men and organizations—quotes like "The measure of who we are is what we do with what we have" and "The only preparation for tomorrow is the right use of today."

I also asked him about a direct quote in an email from the Salvation Army's lawyer sent on June 4 to STB. It was the email in which the lawyer expressed concern about the vibrations caused by the demolition work (demolition work the Salvation Army said it believed wasn't taking place) and how they might cause damage to the display items on the Thrift Store shelves.

Concern for property trumped concern for people—that was the point I wanted to make.

Asked if any discussion was held about closing the store, Deitrick said there had been none "because we did not believe there was any danger going on based on the information we had."

I used slides to show him pictures of some of the victims. And I had photos of the Salvation Army employees who worked in the Thrift Store put up on the screen. Deitrick got confused and had to admit that he really didn't know who was an employee and who was a customer. I thought he came across as clueless and contradictory, although the line of questioning was risky. Deitrick could have promptly turned the tables on me by identifying each employee. The fact that he could not, I felt, undermined his testimony and raised questions about his sincerity and his purported concern for the victims.

I asked if he could "tell me anything about any of these people."

He admitted he could not but added, "That does not mean I did not have care and concern for them. . . . My whole life has been given to the service of people."

"All I can tell you," he said at another point, "is I've had deep concern and compassion for their families, for them. And I've prayed for them over and over during the days."

He said further, "This has been a devastating experience for them, and it crushes me deeply to know that they went through this experience."

In response to his hypocritical testimony, I had difficulty holding back feelings of disbelief, and as I glanced at the jurors, their facial expressions revealed they weren't buying it either. In my view, effective cross-examination allows you to transfer your themes directly into the minds of the jurors. Here, the Salvation Army's "kind and caring" mantra was dismantled by the time Deitrick left the stand, and I had a lot of sound bites I would be able to use in my closing argument. Mongeluzzi and Wigrizer had also contributed to challenging Deitrick's credibility. It appeared as though the jurors had very serious questions about whether the Salvation Army had acted in the best interest of the men and women in the store on that fateful day. The process of changing the benevolent and caring face of the Salvation Army was clearly moving in the right direction.

CHAPTER TWELVE

IT WAS A simple question.

But one I knew he didn't want to answer.

As with Deitrick, I led the cross-examination of Major John Cranford for the plaintiffs. For nearly two hours, I had been firing questions at the retired Salvation Army official directly responsible for the operation of the Thrift Store at 22nd and Market Streets. The store was part of the eastern region he oversaw. From the memos, emails and his deposition testimony, I believed Cranford epitomized the arrogance and ego of the Salvation Army that were at the heart of our case.

It was important for the jury to see that.

"If the store was closed," I asked toward the end of my examination, "can we agree, if the store was not opened as of June 5, no one would have been killed or injured. True?"

First Jack Snyder, the lawyer for the Salvation Army, objected. But Judge Sarmina overruled him. Then Cranford launched into a speech that began with the words, "Who would ever know . . ."

I interrupted him.

"Who would ever know? Excuse me. . . . Can you please answer my question?"

"Can I please finish," said the major. "Who would ever know that STB would have a contractor . . ."

With that, one of the STB lawyers jumped up and objected.

This time the judge upheld the objection. Cranford was not permitted to go down that road. He couldn't make the self-serving and repetitive speech that underlined the Salvation Army's defense. He was trying to come back again to the point that he and other Salvation Army witnesses had adopted as their maxim: if STB had hired a competent contractor to do the demolition, none of this would have happened.

"The Salvation Army building didn't collapse," he had said earlier in his testimony. "It was the Hoagie City building that came down onto the Salvation Army building."

Throughout his testimony he also clung to another Salvation Army position that seemed to fly in the face of the facts. He insisted that he did not ignore any "warnings." In a rather convoluted explanation, he contended there were no warnings. The emails from Marinakos and Simmonds were "statements" that for the most part the Salvation Army did not believe to be true.

He held to that position even after I reintroduced portions of the crucial email correspondence that were now part of the record. I wanted the jury to hear them again. I asked if he had received and/or was familiar with them. He said he had and he was.

These exchanges included the May 10 email in which STB warned that "every minute that passes increases the liability of all parties"; the May 13 email, which read in part, "your response is required to avoid potential damage to subject properties as well as the public"; and the May 15 letter and email characterizing the situation as a "matter of urgency," suggesting the possibility of an "uncontrolled collapse" and stating that "continued delays in responding pose a threat to life, limb and the public safety." The words were shown on a large projector screen so the jury could read them.

Cranford wouldn't budge.

"There were not warnings, sir," he said at one point. At another he replied, "There was no . . . it was not a warning and there was no danger. . . . We had come up with an action plan."

Throughout his testimony, he continued to downplay the original Marinakos email that raised questions about the stability of the Thrift Store building, insisting there was nothing structurally wrong with the property. I then fired off three quick questions, asking if he were a structural engineer, an architect or a demolition and construction expert.

He said he was not. But he insisted there was no need to consult with anyone who was.

"There was no structural engineer needed," he said. "Our building was structurally sound."

None of this surprised me. He had said the same things during his deposition. But I wanted the jurors to hear him. Just as important, I wanted the jurors to see him as he attempted to evade my questions.

He showed up for his court appearance in full uniform, even though he had retired about a year after the wall collapse. He and his wife, the former "Mrs. Major," were living in Myrtle Beach, that lovely South Carolina resort town. To bring out the comfort of his current circumstances, I didn't miss the opportunity of welcoming Major Cranford to Philadelphia and asking him where he lived and whether he was retired.

When I asked about the uniform, he said, "I wear it periodically."

Of course he did.

I then asked if he preferred to be called "mister" or "major."

"I would prefer major," he said.

Of course he would.

That exchange, which came just minutes after I called him to the stand, set the tone for his appearance. And what he said, I hoped, would reinforce the arguments we had been making since the trial opened six weeks earlier. The Salvation Army defense was built on a false premise—a presumption that there was no danger. The facts demonstrated otherwise. Accept, if you will, the argument that the demolition work was shoddy, that STB and Basciano were trying to cut corners, that Simmonds engaged in hyperbole—accept all of that. The bottom line was that the wall collapsed, just as the emails had warned, and the Salvation Army had ignored the potential safety hazards in the process. That was where its responsibility and liability came into play.

Major John Cranford would be one of the last confrontational witnesses we, the plaintiff attorneys, would present to the jury. My hope was to use him to hammer home the central themes in our litigation.

He didn't disappoint. Both his words and his demeanor went to the heart of the case. He and the other Salvation Army officials did nothing to prevent the collapse or to protect their people and customers. Instead, they tried to blame others.

Early in his testimony he said that both the store manager, Margarita Agosto, and her assistant manager had the authority to close the store, implying that if they really felt there was a risk, they should have done so. At another point, in a rather disjointed response to one of my questions, he said that other demolition was going on at the site and it was unclear what Agosto might have been referring to when she expressed concern.

This, of course, contradicted the insistence by Salvation Army officials that they knew nothing about her concern. Nevertheless, Cranford told the jury, "Well, I do know there were sites that were being taken down, and so I am not sure what Margarita was talking about. Was it the demolition that had taken place in those other properties?" At times on cross-examination, when he gave an evasive or incredible response like this one, I would give him an incredulous look as I continued to press for a candid response, and I would say in a taunting tone of voice, "*Now*, Major, Major, Major," until I heard a chuckle from certain jurors, followed by Snyder's vociferous objection.

In this instance, the testimony and evidence already introduced at the trial clearly indicated that the only demolition taking place at the time of the collapse was of the Hoagie City building. I didn't know what to make of his comments, but I felt they undermined his credibility. I hoped the jury saw it the same way.

He said that he had never visited the site and, like other Salvation Army witnesses, that he believed demolition had been put on hold until the roof access question was resolved. This was the access that other evidence and testimony indicated he had no intention of granting. But he skirted that issue, claiming everything was to be addressed in the "action plan" that the Salvation Army was developing with its lawyer and with an architect it had brought in to assess the situation.

In light of the emails that were either "warnings" or "statements," I then asked him if he had ever ordered Pomponi to check with the employees at the store to determine "what's going on."

He said he had not.

I asked if he had ever requested that employees use their cell phones to take pictures of the demolition work and send them to him. Again, he said he had not.

I wanted him to at least acknowledge the "magnitude of risk" that existed in May and June 2013, to accept that there was at least the "potential" for a serious problem. The questions, while based on a common-sense approach that I hoped the jury was adopting, also carried legal ramifications.

Both our claim of intentional infliction of emotional distress and our claim for punitive damages required us to show "extreme and outrageous conduct" in the first phase of the trial. But during that first phase we were prohibited from addressing the severe emotional and physical harm that conduct might have caused. This was the bifurcation the judge had imposed to avoid emotionalizing the liability segment of the trial. But by using the "magnitude of risk" approach, I was able to delve into some aspects of the injuries sustained by Mariya and other victims because they were relevant to our theories of liability.

Specifically, we argued that the Salvation Army's decision not to close the store, in light of the magnitude of the risk of serious bodily injury and/or death to customers and employees, was reckless, extreme and outrageous. As one example, early in the trial, the judge allowed us to briefly discuss the rescue photo with Chief O'Neill—the photo that showed Mariya buried in the rubble. The photo, we contended, was "probative"—that is, it helped prove the magnitude of the risk involved in not closing the store.

This approach was also helpful when our retail expert and another retail expert presented by the Salvation Army testified. Our point was that Salvation Army upper management should have realized that a collapse could injure, maim and kill people. In that regard, I asked Cranford if it was "foreseeable," given the situation, "that people could be buried under the rubble . . . that people could die . . . that people could be permanently injured for the rest of their life."

Jack Snyder objected to the question, but the judge overruled him. Cranford had to answer. I reposed the same question.

"Yes," he replied. This was undoubtedly one of the key admissions in all of his testimony, and later it would form the foundation for my closing arguments.

"Did you think about it?" I said.

Cranford went into a rambling response that again focused on STB, the demolition work and the fact that the City had granted permits allowing the work, implying that all those factors led him to assume the project was safe.

I brought him back to the issue at hand, the potential danger, the foreseeable risk. Did he think about that?

"No," he said.

"I didn't think so," I replied.

Snyder jumped up and objected to my comment. This time the judge upheld the objection and ruled that my words be stricken from the record. I was okay with that. I was confident the jury got the point.

Cranford also testified that he had no independent recollection of the May 22, 2013, Salvation Army staff meeting in which he had rejected his wife's suggestion that the store be closed and employees relocated during the demolition. (Mrs. Cranford would later testify that she also couldn't recall the meeting either. I appreciated her predicament. "Mrs. Major," I felt, was a nice woman who found herself in a difficult position.) Major Cranford, on the other hand, had put himself in that kind of position, and his testimony did little to alleviate the problem. In fact, he told the jury that he believed the discussion about closing the store and relocating the workers was a reference to the Salvation Army's continual quest to find a better location for the Center City store, not a reference to any potential danger posed by the Hoagie City demolition.

We went round and round for most of the morning session in court that day, leading up to my ultimate question, the question that Cranford desperately wanted to avoid: If the store had been closed on June 5, no one would have been killed or injured. Correct?

It was a simple question. Moreover, it pointed to a simple solution that the Salvation Army chose not to pursue. It related to the basic, powerful theory of liability we had developed from the beginning of the case.

And finally, after objections and obfuscation and rambling comments that had little relevance, Major Cranford was forced to answer it.

"That's correct," he said.

We would continue to present our case over the next month. During that time, there was a two-week break to accommodate Judge Sarmina, who had planned a vacation trip long before she was assigned as the trial judge. Both the lawyers and the jurors, I believe, welcomed the respite. By that point there had already been twenty-seven days of testimony.

The hiatus ended on November 15. By November 19 we, the plaintiff attorneys, had wrapped up our case.

Mariya was the last witness we called. With the aid of an interpreter, she basically told the jury that on the dreadful morning she saw no warning signs posted by the Salvation Army, nor was she told by any worker that it was unsafe to shop in the store.

She was there, she said, to take advantage of the "Family Day" discount sales. The store was one of her favorite places to shop, and she often found clothes that she would send home to family and friends in Ukraine. She had been to the store dozens of times and saw nothing different that day. She just wanted to shop.

Given the bifurcation order, that was the extent of what she could say during the first phase of the trial. Yet what she said was important because it helped solidify all of the plaintiffs' claims for intentional misrepresentation, which we needed to prove to hold the Salvation Army legally responsible to pay the entire verdict. There was no question that Mariya's presence in the courtroom, with half of her body missing, helped carry the day on this vital claim. So did her stoic demeanor while testifying.

Notably, she was in court that day in a motorized wheelchair. Her words came out through a device she was required to hold against her throat. Persistent lung problems, months on a respirator and one tracheotomy after another had robbed her of the ability to speak.

Although she couldn't discuss her injuries, I was able to ask her if she could talk without assistance and walk on her own before she entered the Thrift Store that morning.

"Yes," she said with just a hint of emotion.

I was also able to show the jury a picture of her prior to June 5, 2013. It was a photo of her smiling and standing on her own two legs in front of the Philadelphia Museum of Art. It was a picture of a happier time, a better time, a time that was forever lost when the wall came down on the Thrift Store where she was shopping.

The trial lasted another month. Testimony was put on hold for the Christmas/New Year holiday. The defense combined to call about twenty witnesses in an attempt to refute the arguments we had presented. The defendants had their own construction expert (who was paid the staggering amount of $290,000) and their own retail expert. None of this testimony was unexpected, and most of it, I believed, was ineffective.

There had been some talk about a potential settlement after we completed the liability phase of the trial, but the amount would not have satisfied our claims. The Salvation Army had made no firm settlement offer, in part because they were confident they would either win with a defense verdict or do well. The bifurcation of the case was an advantage for the defense in this regard. In such a situation, the defendants can roll the dice, let the testimony come in from the plaintiffs and then try to make a judgment on where the jury might be heading. What I knew was that the STB/Basciano group had placed a relatively small sum of settlement money in an escrow account from the beginning of the case. The Salvation Army had a much more significant insurance policy and loads of assets. Of course, none of the other defendants had anything substantial to add to a potential settlement, so I took the position that the Army had to tender its entire insurance policy, which would be added to the amount already tucked away by the Basciano-related defendants. At this point, some other well-respected Philadelphia judges started to get involved in an effort to reach a settlement, including the Honorable Idee Fox and the Honorable Frederica Massiah-Jackson. Judge Fox was instrumental in getting the parties to seriously contemplate a possible settlement, and Judge Massiah-Jackson offered helpful comments relating to case value assessments.

From my point of view, I was in a unique position. My client, Mariya Plekan, would spend the rest of her life battling the medical and physical problems that resulted from the tragedy. No other plaintiff was in that position. Just about any seven-digit monetary settlement could be construed as a victory for the others. But Mariya's medical bills were astronomical, and the care she would need for the rest of her life carried an astounding price. We were talking tens of millions of dollars. The overall settlement had to be large enough so that her share would cover those costs, and I was not going to sell out. The Salvation Army flatly refused my demands and decided to roll the dice.

Closing arguments began on Tuesday, January 24, 2017. The judge had allotted a specific time for each lawyer. The closings would last two days. I was given ninety minutes during the afternoon of January 24. It was agreed among the lawyers for the plaintiffs that my focus would remain entirely on the Salvation Army.

Closings are the opportunity for lawyers to put all the evidentiary pieces of the puzzle in place. The irony is that we use the same pieces to create different pictures. Then the jury decides which one makes the most sense based on the jurors' view of the evidence and the credibility of the witnesses. I firmly believe that in most cases you don't win your case in your closing argument. Most of the time, the jurors at that point already have a sense of what direction they plan to go with their verdict. Instead, closing arguments are an opportunity to give the jurors important guidance for rendering their findings on a verdict sheet.

It came as no surprise to anyone in the courtroom that Basciano and STB were targeted in the summations of several lawyers. Steve Wigrizer summarized that position best when he said Basciano had taken a "calculated, dangerous chance" when he hired Marinakos, an "inexperienced, incompetent architect," to oversee "a cut-rate demolition contractor."

He also used a quote from inspirational author Roy T. Bennett, who wrote that "every choice comes with a consequence." Basciano, Wigrizer argued, should be held responsible for the consequences of the choices he had made. Wigrizer also argued that all defendants shared responsibility for the tragedy.

My position, which I underscored by showing slides of pieces of testimony, was that the Salvation Army had "multiple opportunities" to address the problem but repeatedly failed to do so. I again clarified that the evidence had established the Salvation Army as clearly the *most* responsible. I also tried to anticipate what Jack Snyder would say and refute it in advance. Consistent with the position I had taken from day one, I continued to place primary and substantial blame on the Salvation Army, and I went out of my way to downplay the potential responsibility of other parties.

Snyder's position, which I expected, was that the Salvation Army was a wonderful charity; how could anyone accuse it of not caring, of somehow being responsible for this horrible and tragic situation?

When he got his chance to speak, he went right down that road, telling the jurors that the Army was engaged in charity and good works and that its officers and personnel would never let anyone enter a "doomed building." His summation came before a packed courtroom that included, in the front row, a bevy of uniformed Salvation Army officials. Snyder claimed it was hard to sit at the defense table day after day and "listen to these allegations against these fine people."

"Do you think that's what the Salvation Army is about?" he asked. Then, with a flourish, he answered his own question. "That's bull and you know it."

My answer, in advance, was to warn the jury about where he might go and underscore our response. I said that people had died and others had been seriously injured because the Salvation Army had failed to do what it so easily could have done.

"They held the keys to the store," I said. "If the store is not open, there's no dispute in this case [because] nobody gets hurt. And so when you listen to this evidence, and in particular, when you listen to Mr. Snyder try to justify things when he gives you his closing remarks, you're gonna have to ask yourself: Have you really been able to explain to me why you didn't look into this at all, to look into really protecting people? Can you really justify why you wouldn't in some form communicate to the people in that store to tell them what's going on so they could protect themselves and the customers? Can you really justify why you wouldn't, just to make things safe for people, just close that store for a period of time to make sure things were safe? Can you really explain that away?"

Those were the key elements in my argument. I tried to come back to those issues throughout my closing, emphasizing that what had happened was "inexcusable" and could easily have been avoided.

"It didn't have to happen," I said at one point.

"There were so many opportunities, members of the jury, so many opportunities for the Salvation Army to just do something to protect these people. Something. They did nothing."

Finally, in what I hoped would be a clear reference to my own client's brief appearance on the witness stand and her inability to speak without the aid of a device, I asked the jurors to be a "voice" for her, for the other victims and for the city itself.

"You are the voice of this community," I said. "You are the voice as jurors in our system that speaks; speak for people who literally can't speak; speak for people who aren't here. Our system of justice gives you, members of the jury, incredible power, very important power. You are our voices. You set standards. You determine what is right. You determine what is wrong. You weigh the evidence."

I added, "This is a very important decision, and I know you all take it very seriously. We ask that your verdict reflect and stand up for those voices that have not been able to speak."

Afterward, I was flattered when certain lawyers in the courtroom complimented me on my performance during the trial. Moreover, I was very pleasantly surprised when Richard Sprague offered unsolicited words of high praise as well.

Closing arguments continued into the next day, setting up what the media would bill as an "oratorical duel" between two high-profile litigators, the legendary Richard Sprague, who represented Basciano, and the master of disaster, Robert Mongeluzzi, who would offer the plaintiffs' rebuttal.

"There's nobody in the case that wanted anybody to die," Sprague told the jury, arguing that the facts and circumstances didn't support the arguments about liability. This was a terrible accident, but not one that Richard Basciano should be held accountable for, he said.

He also told the jury that the plaintiffs "don't want justice." Rather, he said, "they seek revenge." Sprague also pointed out that the plaintiffs had "sneered" at Griffin Campbell and his poor performance as a contractor. He apparently sensed that the jurors appeared to feel a sense of unfairness in light of Campbell and Benschop's incarceration. This was effective; I could sense that jurors thought that Campbell and Benschop got a raw deal.

In his rebuttal, Mongeluzzi said Sprague was "dead wrong" and, among other things, pointed out that while Basciano and STB cut corners and took the lowest bid for what turned out to be shoddy and incompetent demolition work, they had paid $290,000 to a construction expert who testified on their behalf at trial. They were willing to spend hundreds of thousands of dollars on expert witnesses to protect themselves, Mongeluzzi argued, but next to nothing on a demolition project that failed to offer any protection to the people who were killed or injured. The point was clear. If they had spent that kind of money on the demolition project, none of us would have been sitting in court. I liked this rebuttal by Mongeluzzi and especially the manner in which he now focused most of his argument on blaming the Salvation Army. After he had finished and the jurors had been excused, I approached him in front of the other plaintiff lawyers and told him that I thought he was amazing—and he really was.

Closing arguments concluded on a Wednesday afternoon. Judge Sarmina gave the jury the rest of the week off. They would return the following Monday to receive her final instructions on the law and begin deliberations.

After one of the longest trials in Philadelphia Common Pleas Court history, no one knew how long deliberations would take. The jury would have to wade through thousands of pieces of evidence and the testimony of nearly fifty witnesses. There was nothing more we could say. Our work was done. Up to that point, the jurors had been listening. Now was the most challenging portion of the trial—waiting for the jurors to speak.

CHAPTER THIRTEEN

IT DIDN'T take long.

The jury that had heard testimony for fifteen weeks spent less than five hours deliberating before reaching a decision. Word spread through the courthouse late on Tuesday afternoon, January 31.

There was a verdict.

Even Judge Sarmina seemed surprised. One newspaper report said she appeared "stunned" by the fact the jury had decided so quickly.

Trying to analyze jury deliberations is as inexact a science as trying to select jurors. Everyone has a theory. Most pundits would tell you that a quick verdict in a case this involved could mean only one thing: the jury found little reason to debate any of the issues or arguments presented by the plaintiffs and defendants. The question was which arguments the panel accepted. From my personal experience, juries that have deliberated for several hours, as opposed to several days, usually favor the plaintiff.

With people still scurrying into the courtroom, the panel of seven men and five women was brought in to announce its findings. It took nearly fifteen minutes for the jury foreman to read off the results contained in a seven-page, thirty-six-question verdict sheet.

The first question on that sheet was: "Do you find that The Salvation Army was negligent?"

The answer to that question and virtually every other question that followed was "yes." In that moment, I felt vindicated. My client would find justice at the end of this painstaking journey. The jury had done the right thing.

I always keep a verdict sheet that I check off as the jury's finding are read. I felt myself checking off the sheet with a new kind of intensity as each question relating to the Salvation Army's responsibility was answered in the affirmative.

The jury had found every defendant liable, every defendant responsible and accountable, though the percentages of responsibility varied quite a bit. The jury also decided that all but Griffin Campbell had demonstrated negligent and outrageous conduct that showed "a reckless indifference to the interests of others."

Our arguments had been accepted in total. What's more, when it came to assessing percentages of responsibility, the jury ruled that the Salvation Army was *most* responsible for the deaths and injuries of those who had been shopping in the Thrift Store that fateful morning. The jury set the Army's liability at a whopping seventy-five percent! STB was assigned thirteen percent, Basciano and Marinakos five percent each. Finally, the jury found that Benschop and Campbell, the only people who had been criminally prosecuted and convicted, were each only *one* percent responsible. For the Salvation Army employees who were killed or injured (and who were prohibited by law from suing their employer), the jury found Basciano and STB each thirty-four percent liable, Marinakos thirty percent and Campbell and Benschop again one percent each. In sum, I believed this jury had completely understood the evidence and had used superb judgment in rendering a verdict and allocating fault.

It was a staggering decision. As I looked around the courtroom, I saw its impact in the faces of Jack Snyder and the other members of the Salvation Army defense team. It was a look of disappointment, shock and disbelief. John Hare, the well-respected appellate lawyer for the Salvation Army, was likely contemplating the viable avenues for a successful appeal. Indeed, even though Judge Sarmina had done a masterful job of handling the complex legal issues in the case, it would have come as no surprise that upholding the verdict would be as challenging as getting it in the first place.

Even though the plaintiffs' evidence had focused on the responsibility of all parties, the jurors had been able to properly analyze the evidence that proved the Salvation Army's substantial role in this catastrophe. The decision to sue the charity, and moreover to emphasize that it was a business with the same responsibilities and obligations as any other retail store, had paid off. For the first time in almost four years, I let out a sigh of relief. My client and the other victims now had the opportunity to be properly compensated.

The Salvation Army, according to its publicly available 2015 annual report (the latest report at that time), had an astronomical $14.8 billion in assets. It claimed $2.7 billion in revenue for the year, with slightly more than twenty percent of that revenue coming from its thrift stores. We intended to get that information to the jury during the next phase of the trial and to ask the jury to base its financial damage awards in part on those numbers. At this point in the case, however, the jurors knew *nothing* about the Army's massive wealth. But the defendants knew we would now be able to put that information to use.

The game had changed.

Now the defendants had to decide whether they wanted the jury to attach actual dollar amounts to its liability findings, or whether it might be smarter to work out a settlement.

With a gag order still in place, none of us could comment about the liability verdict. But there was more important business to address. Judge Sarmina, determined to keep things in motion, ordered the damages phase of the trial to begin that Friday. We would each be permitted to make a brief opening statement and then the process of calling witnesses would begin again.

This time the focus wouldn't be on why and how the wall had collapsed. Instead, the jurors would hear what had happened to the people buried in the rubble. These were horrible, gut-wrenching stories that would add emotion and pathos to the process. They were stories about the pain and suffering of victims who, testimony would show, were alive and suffering for six, seven or eight hours before they died, victims whose necks were broken, whose bodies were twisted and compressed, whose arms were found outstretched as if struggling to find a way out. And they would get to hear about Mariya.

None of it was pretty. All of it would be used to urge the jury to come up with both compensatory and punitive damage amounts. The jury would be asked to assess the loss of potential revenue and earnings of the victims. That would relate to the compensatory damages. And it would also be asked to set a financial number on the pain and suffering of those who had survived and on the loss to the family members of those who had perished. This would be the punitive damage assessment.

Those were the stakes as the second phase of the trial began.

Not surprisingly, word came from the defense camp that they would now like to discuss a possible monetary settlement. I continued to lead the plaintiffs' team in determining our approach to a settlement. My position was that I wouldn't even come to a settlement table unless the Salvation Army agreed to immediately tender all of its substantial insurance policy. Basciano and STB, as mentioned earlier, had already put up their money, but their insurance, combined with the Salvation Army's insurance policy, wasn't enough from where I stood. Quite frankly, I felt the Salvation Army should have tendered its money at the start of the trial, as Basciano/STB had done, and I wasn't about to discuss a settlement without that commitment.

Opening arguments and testimony in the damages phase of the trial began on Friday, February 3. My focus in my opening remarks was on Mariya's injuries, her ongoing medical condition and the fact that she would need full-time, round-the-clock nursing care for the rest of her life.

I told the jury she had been described as the "Miracle on Market Street" after being pulled alive from the rubble after suffering thirteen hours of horror and pain, but that this particular "miracle" would end in a nightmare.

She had already undergone thirty surgeries, was in constant pain and had lost the bottom half of her body. I described the ghastly "maggot therapy" (using sterilized microorganisms) that she endured to attack the infections that were racking her body, and the number of times she had gone into "septic shock" as a result of her injuries and infections.

As important, I said, was the loss of her dignity and self-reliance. She could no longer do the things that she loved. She could no longer take walks and visit the historic sites of her adopted city. She could no longer get out of bed without the use of a mechanical lift and the assistance of a nurse's aide. She could no longer get down on her hands and knees to play with her granddaughter.

All of that had been taken away from her, replaced by fear, uncertainty, frustration, pain and anger.

"Physically and mentally," I told the jurors, Mariya Plekan will live with the horrific results of June 5, 2013, "for the rest of her life." Now it was up to them to determine what that was worth, what financial figure could be placed on the damages that had been inflicted.

With that I returned to a theme that had been part of our argument from day one: When the Salvation Army opened its doors for business on June 5, 2013, it was saying to its customers that it was safe to come in and shop.

Mariya and the other customers who entered the store that morning trusted the Salvation Army. "They believed in them," I said. "And those people at the Salvation Army betrayed that trust and took advantage of it. And what punitive damages is allowing you to do is evaluate three basic things: The conduct, the harm, and something else called net worth. Because the idea is, unfortunately in our society, that certain defendants are not deterred from engaging in bad conduct unless it hits them in . . . the pocketbook. Money. That's all that matters to certain people. That's all they understand, and so the law in Pennsylvania, under punitive damage analysis, allows you to consider the net worth."

Of course, I wanted to finally reveal to the jurors the enormous wealth of the Army. That would eventually be part of our presentation, but the judge had ruled I couldn't use that information in my opening remarks.

The plaintiffs' strategy in this phase of the trial was to lay out in detail the pain and suffering. The plaintiffs' lawyers would use the testimony of victims who had survived, of family members who had lost loved ones and of rescue workers and medical experts who would explain what they had seen and done or what autopsies and body placement in the rubble had indicated.

The six victims who had died had experienced unspeakable injuries. It was a terrible thing for family members to hear those details, but it was important for the jury to understand what Bob Mongeluzzi, in his opening statement, referred to as the "enormity of that harm, the enormity of that disaster, the enormity of the horror."

Mongeluzzi discussed nine plaintiffs in the case, including the estates of Juanita Harmon and Anne Bryan, two of the people who had died. In his opening he told about Juanita Harmon, the seventy-five-year-old retired secretary, the loving mother and grandmother. He told the jury she had "lived six to eight hours in the rubble, trapped, her body compressed, her neck broken."

As one of the first plaintiff witnesses, he called her fifty-nine-year-old son, Andre, to the stand. Andre Harmon narrated a slide show about his mother, who had raised four sons on her own. He explained how she doted on her grandchildren, how she loved life and how her family missed her every day.

"None of us will see her again," he said, "hear her laugh again. As a family there's a hole there. . . . I don't know what people are talking about when they say there's going to be some closure. There is none." Mongeluzzi did a terrific job representing his clients in this early part of the damages phase of the trial.

The plan was for this kind of testimony to continue. We intended to present the jury with a description of each victim, offer comments from the loved ones of those who had died and testimony about the horror and suffering from those who had survived. Mariya would be our last witness. She would provide a firsthand account of that horror, of what it was like to be under that rubble, wondering and hoping and praying. Her experience would be the closest the jury would come to hearing what it was like for those who had died.

But it never got that far.

Settlement negotiations began shortly after the damages phase opened and after the Salvation Army agreed to my demand that it tender the whole of its significant insurance policy. Of course, I wanted more than the Salvation Army's available insurance proceeds. From my point of view, the Army would have to dig into its own pockets to come up with enough additional money to make this litigation go away.

We, the attorneys in the case, would meet after the day's trial session had ended. The meetings were in the offices of Jerry Roscoe, a lawyer who had been appointed mediator by agreement of all parties. Roscoe, who worked for an independent alternative-dispute-resolution firm, was a well-respected and highly intelligent mediator who had effectively worked many high-profile and complicated cases.

During negotiations the plaintiff attorneys would sit in one room and the defense attorneys in another. Roscoe would shuttle between the two groups, providing information in an effort to facilitate a resolution. The specific conversations of the negotiations are private, but the process moved rather quickly. Roscoe came to the plaintiff attorneys with an offer above the Salvation Army's insurance tender that had been added to the money that the Basciano-related defendants had coughed up from the beginning. Of course, the marginal amount of insurance coverage available through the other defendants, such as Marinakos, was also added to the pot. The offer was substantial and, I believed, much more than many plaintiff attorneys thought might have been possible when they first entered the case. There was pressure on me from certain plaintiff lawyers to agree to the number.

One of the other lawyers nearly jumped across the table when I suggested the offer was still not enough. In fact, I thought the settlement would have to be larger if Mariya were to get the care she needed.

Sensing that the defendants had reached their limit as to what they would offer, I instructed Liz to pack up. We were going to leave the negotiations and head back to court to continue with the damages trial. One of the other plaintiff lawyers, who had emerged as the leader for the larger block of attorneys, asked to speak with me privately in a separate room before I left—he wanted me to be "reasonable."

As I listened to that lawyer, apart from the others, I thought about what my mentor, the late Jim Beasley, had always taught me: Quoting George Bernard Shaw, he would say that "progress depends on the unreasonable man." Indeed, Beasley had those words inscribed on the wall of his law firm's handsome library at 12th and Walnut Streets in Philadelphia.

The lawyer and I had talked for only a few minutes when there was a knock on the door. Now there was an indication that the settlement offer had been substantially increased to meet my demand. With that representation, I decided I would stay. After we rejoined the other plaintiff attorneys, we soon had a deal—a Pennsylvania record $227 million global settlement!

The settlement was announced on February 8, 2017. We gathered in court that day for what would have been the fourth day of testimony in the damages phase of the trial, but the buzz in the courthouse that morning made it clear that the case had settled. All the parties began to arrive in the sixth-floor courtroom around noon. The body language and looks on the faces of the lawyers and plaintiffs sent out a clear signal that it was over.

Mariya, in her motorized wheelchair, reached up and hugged Nancy Winkler. Both women had tears in their eyes. It was always obvious that Ms. Winkler and her husband, Jay Bryan, were devastated by their loss. While no settlement or guilty verdict would ever bring back their daughter or heal the wound in their hearts, this might provide at least some measure of justice.

The jury was called into the room. Judge Sarmina told them the trial was over, that a settlement had been reached. She thanked them for their service and told them this outcome couldn't have happened without them. She was on the verge of tears as well—this trial had dominated all of our lives for many months.

"The fact is that your findings in your liability verdict were pivotal in these claims being able to settle," she said.

The jury's liability verdict had forced the Salvation Army to the settlement table. The Army and its lawyers had decided not to take a second chance on the jury. It was better to settle than to allow the same men and women who had found them seventy-five percent responsible for the tragedy to place a dollar figure on the suffering of each of the victims.

Under the terms of the settlement, we were not permitted to disclose the exact amount each party contributed. But Joe Slobodzian, the *Philadelphia Inquirer* reporter who had covered the trial from day one, publicly reported that the Salvation Army was providing the bulk of the cash—$200 million. Without commenting on the accuracy of his story one way or the other, I can say that I never spoke with Slobodzian about the breakdown of the settlement contributions, and to this day I do not know his source. However, as everyone in the business knows, Slobodzian is a very respected reporter.

We held a press conference at the Thomas R. Kline School of Law at Drexel University about ten blocks from the site of the Thrift Store. I decided to have a separate press conference, apart from the other plaintiff lawyers, because I wanted to ensure that Mariya got the news media coverage she deserved. Chief O'Neill, who had found Mariya in the rubble, sat next to her that afternoon. The next day, Mariya's picture appeared on the front page of the *Philadelphia Inquirer*—she was no longer the forgotten victim, and Liz and I rejoiced at Mariya's deserved recognition.

Mariya was physically and emotionally unable to speak at the press conference. The settlement had ended the litigation but did little to alleviate her suffering. When reporters asked how she felt, her friend Dariya Tareb responded for her. She had been by her side through most of her ordeal and was sitting with her that day.

"To be happy is very difficult for her," she said. "She lost half her body."

That was the hard reality.

"Before this happened, she was completely healthy," I said.

At another press conference in Bob Mongeluzzi's law office, most of the other plaintiff attorneys simultaneously offered their comments about the case, i.e., the settlement and what it all meant. Most agreed that it was a warning to others who might find themselves in the same situation, a warning not to cut corners and, above all else, to consider the safety of those who might be placed in harm's way.

The attorneys added that it was the "largest settlement in Pennsylvania state court history." Yep, it sure was, and I was flattered by objective participants, such as Jerry Roscoe, who recently expressed to me that I was the primary reason the settlement had reached such an astronomical number.

In the wake of the settlement, Max Mitchell of the Philadelphia *Legal Intelligencer* published an article on February 9, 2017, that addressed the issue:

"Kline and Specter attorney, Andy Stern, who did not take part in the press conference with Mongeluzzi, Wigrizer, Roth and others, but was also a lead attorney in the case, said his strategy of focusing exclusively on the Salvation Army—a nationally recognized charity—was risky, but ultimately paid off," the article read. It went on to quote me on the topic. "'If the jurors don't like that, you are the lawyer who gets attached to that theory of liability and any time you're in court, it is not just the witnesses' credibility that's assessed, your credibility is critical,' Stern said. 'But contrary to [the Salvation Army's] motto of doing the most good, they did the most harm.'"

In the end, the jury decision that found the Salvation Army seventy-five percent liable validated our position. Nothing anyone else said really mattered.

Neither Jack Snyder nor the Salvation Army officials in court on the final day offered any comment to the media, but a spokesman for the charity, Phil Pagliaro, provided reporters with a statement that said, "Our deepest sympathy remains with the victims and their families through this extremely difficult time. We are praying for the healing of our community."

It seems that "thoughts and prayers" is a common expression used when bad things happen to good people. But those words, usually spoken after the fact, do little to alleviate the problem. More important, they ring hollow when coming from those responsible for the problem in the first place.

While the settlement was reached in February, it was several more months before the money was disbursed. Jerry Roscoe, who had served as mediator, was now assigned the task of arbitrator. He would preside over a series of private hearings in which each of the plaintiffs, with their attorneys, would present a case for how much they should receive of the $227 million. The hearings began on March 8 and ran through May 3.

The consensus, reported in several media stories, was that Mariya would be awarded the largest amount because of her grievous suffering and injuries as well as her continuing medical needs. That had seemed to be a given. But when the arbitration process began, we found ourselves fighting another battle. It was the death cases versus Mariya Plekan— and who was worth more.

The cold and calculating questions that had remained in the background now became the focal point: How much was a life worth? And was a life lost worth more than the suffering and future needs of someone who had survived without the bottom half of a body? As the plaintiff lawyers advocated for their clients, arguments once again became heated and confrontational.

During the lengthy arbitration process, Mariya's health began to deteriorate further. She was rushed to the hospital on two different occasions. She needed more intensive, round-the-clock care, care that was not possible at the nursing home where she was living. Her medical costs had already exceeded $17 million. While insurance covered most of that, she already had a substantial monetary lien being asserted against her. What's more, Medicare had told the nursing home it would no longer cover her costs.

It was important that we get fair and full compensation for her and that the cash be promptly disbursed. The process was tedious, but by the end of May 2017, Jerry Roscoe had made his decisions. Mariya would receive $95.6 million, the biggest individual settlement in the case and the biggest single-plaintiff recovery in Pennsylvania history. By agreement, this was a binding arbitration, and so there was no avenue for appeal. Even better, Mariya would have more than enough to deal with her expected medical expenses and to create a home for her and her family.

The bad news was that the disbursement of the money was held up. There were issues with the settlement release, and the defendants would not sign off until all parties were on board. This caused the first delay. And then, in what I found incredible, I was informed that some plaintiff attorneys were considering a request for a "common fee" in order to obtain more money than they would receive from their individual client contingent-fee agreements—a pursuit that is not even permitted under the law in Pennsylvania.

Any delay, at this point, threatened Mariya's life. To say I was bothered by this development doesn't begin to explain the frustration and disappointment I was feeling. This was a case about human suffering and death and holding people and institutions accountable. We had succeeded in establishing accountability and achieving a record recovery— what was this latest maneuver about?

Essentially it was a battle over the spoils, using arguments that I believed were not grounded in the facts or objective legal strategies. We didn't have time for that kind of posturing. For Liz Crawford and myself, this was about the care and medical attention that our surviving and grievously injured client—*our only client in the case*—desperately needed.

I sought legal advice from several well-respected members of the bar as to what could be done. Early in June 2017, we filed an emergency motion with the court to compel payment. This type of motion led to a separate court proceeding before a different judge.

Our filing read in part: "Despite the fact all of the binding allocations had already been made by Mr. Roscoe, as a matter of professional courtesy, [we] attempted to work with all Plaintiffs' counsel to get the Release signed as soon as possible. However, one of the plaintiff lawyers has insisted on taking certain positions relating to requests for revisions to language in the Release, and despite continued efforts by the undersigned, it is apparent that the issues will not be promptly resolved in the near future."

From there, I went on to detail some of the medical issues that were now putting Mariya's life in jeopardy, the mounting costs of her medical treatment and the fact that the nursing home where she was living could not provide the care she needed. Our motion was supported by well-credentialed medical expert reports and records.

The records we submitted included, among other things, Mariya's emergency trips to the Hospital of the University of Pennsylvania on May 10 and June 2. On May 10, she was admitted with "severe sepsis and chronic respiratory failure with hypoxia." She wasn't getting enough oxygen. On June 2, she had kidney stones removed and was treated for a life-threatening infection known as pyelonephritis.

Another major problem was that secretions continued to build up in her windpipe. The condition was described as "severe tracheobronchitis." The secretions had to be suctioned out of her body on a regular basis, five or six times a day. If not, she would find it difficult, sometimes impossible, to breathe.

A medical report from one of our consulting physicians noted that "it is essential that her suctioning needs be provided by a respiratory therapist." As the report said, her current nursing facility was not equipped to provide that kind of professional treatment. The report also noted that because of several episodes in which she could not breathe, Mariya was living with "unconscionable fear, dread and the sensations of impending doom."

"Most recently," our emergency motion added, "the nursing home in West Philadelphia where she has been living . . . has *denied* all of her skilled therapy services that have been recommended by HUP as a result of non-payment by Medicare."

In conclusion, I argued that Mariya's "health and welfare is at stake, and she needs to be transferred from her current living facility as soon as possible in order to receive the proper twenty-four-hour skilled nursing and other medical care." I said the "continued delay" in her receiving the money awarded in the binding arbitration process was creating dangerous and unnecessary medical risks. I also noted that, in addition to the Department of Welfare's lien of close to $1 million against her, the "type of care and treatment that she requires will necessitate considerable up-front expenses."

The settlement she had been awarded would clearly cover those costs—but only if she were given the money! Some plaintiffs filed legal arguments opposing our position. Our motion was summarily denied by a court order, without prejudice, because the situation was not deemed to be an "emergency." Liz and I were surprised. But I was most taken aback by the obvious smirk I saw on the face of one plaintiff attorney when we were given a copy of the order in the presence of all trial counsel.

Soon, because of her need for immediate medical care, Mariya had to take out a loan for over half a million dollars.

When I heard what the interest rate would be for this loan, I was disgusted. While we had at times experienced heated disagreements during the case and especially during the arbitration process, at this point I was particularly upset. Once again, I have no problem with aggressive advocacy that is professionally motivated and based on rational client-related objectives, but when it goes beyond the pale and becomes personal, that's another matter.

Another point of contention was the fact that some of the other plaintiff lawyers were attempting to place all the settlement money from the defendants into one common fund—a "Qualified Settlement Fund"—and each plaintiff would then request their individual allocation from one trustee. With the improper "common fee" threat still lingering—which risked my client's money being held up for many months—I had no alternative but to object to this manner of payment. I also had to hire Kristen Behrens, an accomplished trusts and estates lawyer who specializes in special needs trusts and post-litigation planning, among other matters. She was a voice of reason and objectivity in the mix of opinionated lawyers. Because she questioned whether this type of trust was in the best interest of Mariya, or even necessary in the first place, I was able to avoid having Mariya's money placed into a Qualified Settlement Fund.

The dispute wasn't resolved until July of 2017, when another hearing was held and the holdout lawyers, including Bob Mongeluzzi, finally announced they would not seek a common fee in response to a question posed by Judge Matthew D. Carafiello, who is the Administrative Judge of the Philadelphia Orphans Court.

We continued to work to get a fully executed release and obtain the money Mariya critically required. To expedite the process of securing a signed release, I volunteered to drive to Rockview State Prison in central Pennsylvania to request Sean Benschop's signature. Many people in the courtroom doubted that Benschop would agree to sign. I rushed out of the courthouse and, after a three-hour drive in the pouring rain, arrived just minutes before the prison's visiting hours ended. As I walked into the visiting room, I saw Sean, who had a kind smile on his face. He remembered Liz and me, and his greeting was warm, probably because we had always been polite to him and had not tried to focus the blame on him. After I explained the situation, Sean gladly agreed to sign the release.

Finally, in August 2017, we were able to obtain the settlement money. None of the money, of course, would replace what Mariya had lost, nor would it fill the void in the lives of family members and friends who lost loved ones in the disaster. Justice, closure, satisfaction, revenge—attach any word you want to the outcome of this case and it still doesn't address the pain and suffering, the agony and loss.

A few days after the settlement was announced, *Inquirer* reporter Joe Slobodzian was able to interview one of the jurors in the case. Her name was Syreeta Harmon. She was a forty-three-year-old social worker and mother of five. In the interview, she offered some interesting insights into the case and the witnesses. She said she was less than impressed with Basciano, whom she compared to an actor playing a role. She thought Marinakos was an "obvious opportunist." And she felt Campbell and Benschop had been "scapegoats."

Of greater significance, she was most disappointed in the Salvation Army. "As a Christian woman of faith, it was really disheartening that they didn't think enough of their employees to include them in the know," she said.

It was clear she had gotten the point of our arguments. And, from the verdict, it was clear the other jurors had as well. To this day, people familiar with the case cannot believe how cooperative, hard-working and dedicated our jury was. For a span of almost five months, this jury showed up each day ready to work, and in the end they all discharged their duties with fidelity and integrity.

Finally, in the news article, Ms. Harmon was asked about the $227 million settlement.

Her reply put it all in perspective.

"Still not enough," she said.

EPILOGUE

On June 5, 2018, the memorial park at 22nd and Market Streets was formally dedicated and opened to the public. Political officials, members of police, fire and rescue units and the friends and families of those who perished five years earlier were on hand to mark the occasion and remember those who had died.

Private donations, a grant from the City and the donation of the land by the Salvation Army made it possible. The small, neatly appointed park includes a stone memorial with the names of those who were buried under the rubble that day.

The one exception was Mariya Plekan. She spent thirteen hours in a squat position under that pile of concrete, metal and other debris I still cannot begin to comprehend how she was able to do that. Her injuries are unimaginable; she suffered and continues to suffer because of the tragedy. But her name will not be mentioned at a site that marks one of the greatest catastrophes in the history of the city of Philadelphia. I made the request to the appropriate people that, somewhere in the park, her name be listed, but my request was denied.

True, Mariya didn't die, but her physical presence as the most severely injured survivor completely changed the complexion, direction and ultimately the outcome of the civil litigation. Moreover, like other surviving victims, she deserves some recognition in that memorial. Mariya Plekan was one of the significant reasons the Salvation Army was held substantially accountable.

Today, adjacent to the memorial park, is a paved surface parking lot. Richard Basciano's Gateway project is just a footnote to the public tragedy. Less than two blocks west on Market Street, a new commercial development is in the works. The site includes properties at 2324–28 Market Street that Basciano sold in 2015, two years after the wall collapse. These properties include the building he wanted to trade with the

Salvation Army for the Thrift Store site. The sale price of the 2324–28 Market Street location was, according to City records, $3.25 million dollars.

If the Salvation Army had taken him up on his offer . . .

Mr. Basciano died on May 1, 2017, as the arbitration process was nearing completion. His obituary in the *New York Times* appeared under the headline: "Richard Basciano, Times Square Pornography Magnate, Dies at 91."

The obituary went on to describe him as a "sultan of smut"; it detailed his vast real estate holdings and noted that he had made millions when the Times Square area was remade into a commercial and tourist destination.

Adding that he "did not fare as well as a developer in Philadelphia," the article provided details about the wall collapse, the lawsuit and the ultimate verdict. One of his lawyers told the *Times*, "His concern about the accident and those killed and seriously injured weighed upon him very much, and no doubt took a toll on his health." As Shakespeare wrote in *Hamlet*, "Conscience doth make cowards of us all."

Griffin Campbell continues to serve the fifteen-to-thirty-year sentence imposed following his criminal trial, although both his lawyer and the local branch of the NAACP are working on an appeal to have that conviction overturned. They cite the civil jury's decision to hold him only one percent liable as part of their argument. They also hope to use testimony from Basciano, other STB officials and the Salvation Army to bolster their claim that Campbell didn't get a fair trial and was unjustly scapegoated by the District Attorney.

Campbell was described as the "forgotten victim" of the Salvation Army wall-collapse tragedy in a sympathetic article written by *Inquirer* reporter Inga Saffron after the verdict in the civil trial was announced. The Pulitzer Prize–winning journalist wrote that Campbell "didn't run away from the site after it erupted in a mushroom cloud of bricks and dust, but stayed to help dig out the victims. He didn't seek immunity from prosecution as architect Plato Marinakos Jr. did. He didn't take the Fifth like Basciano, or accept a plea deal, as excavator Sean Benschop chose to do. Campbell naively believed that the judicial system would recognize he was a bit player in a terrible accident and would punish him accordingly. Instead, he was given a sentence of 15 to 30 years."

Articulating the position that the NAACP has rallied behind, Saffron wrote that "as long as Campbell's sentence stands, it will send a message that there are two types of justice—one for those with money and connections, and one for those without." To be clear, I have no criticism of the individual Assistant District Attorneys who were assigned to prosecute the criminal case—they were doing their job in an ethical manner. Seth Williams's decision, as the District Attorney, to focus solely on Campbell and Benschop, and to prosecute them to the fullest extent, raises a number of issues that are still under scrutiny.

Plato Marinakos, much to the chagrin of many people, continues to work as an architect in Philadelphia, although Nancy Winkler and her husband Jay Bryan have raised serious questions about how and why he remains licensed.

The couple and their attorney, Bob Mongeluzzi, held a press conference in December 2017 to draw attention to the issue. Jay Bryan had filed a complaint with the state board that licenses architects in 2015, asking that Marinakos's license be denied. The board has declined to comment on any ongoing investigation, but at this writing Marinakos is still licensed to work as an architect in the Commonwealth of Pennsylvania. Bryan raised questions about the board and its licensing process at the news conference held in Mongeluzzi's law office.

"Their mission is to protect public safety, and this was a colossal failure to protect public safety by a licensed architect who was intimately involved with the project from beginning to end," Mongeluzzi said, according to an *Inquirer* article published in January 2018.

Mongeluzzi went on to describe Marinakos's substantial role in the collapse as deliberately creating a danger to the Salvation Army property. It is evident that even to the present day, Marinakos is still viewed by some as the primary cause of the death, injury and destruction surrounding that horrific day.

Mariya Plekan continues to struggle with medical issues that will never be resolved, but she is receiving intensive, round-the-clock care that has made her life livable, if not always enjoyable. More than any other victim, she continues to suffer the results of the arrogance, pride and hubris of those responsible for the tragedy. Along with Liz Crawford, I was honored to be her voice through the legal chaos and challenges that followed. I have also become much more than Mariya's lawyer. She is my friend, and I have been told on more than one occasion that Mariya considers me to be part of her wonderful family.

And while we felt at times that the media had missed or failed to highlight the position we had taken and Mariya's crucial role in the drama, this dramatically changed when Joe Slobodzian, the reporter who covered the Market Street Building Collapse trial on a daily basis, wrote an extensive article in the June 3, 2018, Sunday edition of the *Philadelphia Inquirer*. The article was published to mark the fifth anniversary of the notorious building collapse. Under a front-page headline that read, "THE WILL TO LIVE / Buried in the rubble for 13 hours with grievous injuries, Mariya Plekan endures," the piece went on to describe not just Mariya's struggle, but her amazing ability to find hope, joy and love in the aftermath of the tragedy that changed her life forever. The well-written article speaks for itself and mirrors many of the points I have made here. Most important, however, is that Mariya is no longer the forgotten victim in this tragedy. There was also a front-page photograph of Mariya, taken by David Swanson, that is the best post-building-collapse picture of her I have ever seen.

Mariya is now living in a suburb of Philadelphia with her daughter and grandchildren. Her son, who lives nearby, has recently married, and he and his wife, Ulyana Zatorska, are constant visitors. Mariya's children hope to establish permanent residency in the United States. Her two-story, handsomely appointed home is on a corner lot in the suburban housing development. Two blocks away is a strip mall. It is a beautiful slice of middle America, several miles and light years away from her old North Philadelphia neighborhood.

Mariya moves easily around the house in her motorized wheelchair and often spends time in the kitchen helping prepare meals. She has a trained nurse/home health care professional to attend to her daily medical needs, and her home is equipped with the medical equipment she needs to survive. She and her family are also actively involved in a nearby Ukrainian American church.

Her favorite place is her garden, just outside her home, where the family plants vegetables. She enjoys tending to the garden and just smelling the flowers—simple things that many of us take for granted. Things that she will never take for granted.

Her daughter recently gave birth to a baby boy. Mariya now has two grandchildren living with her and smiles often when they are around.

She is one tough lady, and her resilience and determination are astonishing. Although she enjoys the substantial monetary fruits of her fight for life and justice in Philadelphia, she would give every nickel back in a heartbeat if her previous lifestyle could be miraculously restored. When she is asked about the thirteen hours under the rubble, she is quick to thank those who rescued her and praise the doctors, nurses and other health aides who helped her get where she is today. Mariya also never forgets those who did not survive the shocking ordeal, as well as the surviving family and friends who continue to grieve the loss of their loved ones.

But what kept her going during those thirteen hours in hell, she says, was the thought of her children back home in Ukraine.

"I am their mother," she said. "I knew they needed me. I knew I had to survive."

ACKNOWLEDGMENTS

SPECIAL THANKS to my co-author, George Anastasia, for his objective account of this extraordinary story based on his tireless review of all of the depositions, discovery materials and trial-related documentation. George's insights and superb writing style substantially contributed to my goal of composing an accurate depiction of the people and events surrounding the disaster. To Liz Crawford, my professional colleague and co-counsel, who was never too busy to locate relevant documentation and provide her valuable editing techniques before our final draft was sent to our experienced publisher at Camino, Edward Jutkowitz. To Richard Sprague for his sage advice and helpful review, and to Avery Rome, a very talented and perceptive writer. To Pat Croce and his intuitive guidance that allowed me to better grasp the big-picture objectives of this storyline. To the remarkable Mariya Plekan and her family, thanks for your perseverance, your patience and your faith in me. And finally to my beautiful and gifted wife, Gwen, my true love and inspiration, for all of her unyielding encouragement and affection in our 30 years of marriage.